interior inspirations

Roger Banks-Pye

COLEFAX AND FOWLER

interior inspirations

Roger Banks-Pye

COLEFAX AND FOWLER

Photography by **James Merrell**

Bulfinch Press
Little, Brown and Company
Boston New York Toronto London

First North American Edition

First published in Great Britain in 1997 by
Ryland Peters & Small, London, England

ISBN 0-8212-2333-X
Library of Congress Catalog Card Number
96-78531

Bulfinch Press is an imprint and trademark of
Little, Brown and Company (Inc.)
Published simultaneously in Canada by
Little, Brown & Company (Canada) Limited

Produced by Mandarin Offset
PRINTED IN HONG KONG

$\mathcal{C}$ontents

Foreword

I first met Roger Banks-Pye in 1989. After a long search I had found my perfect London house in Egerton Crescent in Knightsbridge. I turned to Tom Parr of Colefax and Fowler for advice on how to redo it. He entrusted the project to Roger Banks-Pye. In every major city where I have a home, I have taken the trouble to work with someone who will capture the spirit of the place. I sensed almost immediately that Roger Banks-Pye would give me the perfect interpretation of English style for this London house. We had good raw material: a five-story, white stucco-fronted, late-19th-century Victorian house in one of the most elegant terraces in Knightsbridge. It didn't look so bad when I bought it, but it was full of chintzy fabrics, and a man cannot live in a house full of flowers. I didn't want a simple rendition of classic English style. I wanted something more aggressive and strong.

From our first meeting, I sensed that here was a man who would have great sympathy for the project. Roger had a meticulous eye for detail, a great sensitivity for beautiful objects, a natural instinct for scale, and an artist's understanding for light. He had a feeling for formality, but it was tempered with a kind of eccentricity that is the essence of English style. The conservatory, dressed up as it is in bold blue-and-white cotton gingham, is so typical: not at all grand in the conventional sense—witty, light, and very chic. A less imaginative person might have felt intimidated by the formality of the house and the crescent into doing something very stiff. I can't imagine anything less appropriate. Roger never overworked this project. To be relaxed and confident enough to stick your neck out is the sign of a real master.

His sense of a room took in every possible dimension: he somehow managed to make it both eclectic and clean, grand but also intimate, cozy and refined. He had a feeling of color and proportion that was very exciting. We put great dark pieces of heavy furniture in quite small rooms. We dressed dark spaces in bright colors. We broke all the rules with this house. He created a dining room that can be used to host both formal and family dinners with equal ease. But while we had fun breaking the rules, we always kept as a priority the need for women to look and feel beautiful when they sat in any of these rooms.

Roger might have had an adventurous spirit when it came to choosing objects and colors and creating the proportions, but they were never chosen without thought and care for their setting; they were never strange or uneasy. First and foremost, he had an almost instinctive understanding of what I wanted to achieve with this house. London is where I relax: I read, I go to movies, I see friends, and we have dinners *in famiglia*. Sometimes I just go to bed early with a plate of pasta and a biography I have been saving for weeks. Roger's challenge was to achieve the perfect place for all of this.

Sometimes it can be easier to create a showpiece. To make a home is a more exacting challenge. Roger proved himself psychologist, friend and sometimes miracle worker. For example, I told him I needed a place full of light and I was determined to create a feeling of large spaces out of rooms that were really built to be cosy ones. Egerton Crescent has good light, but London townhouses are not noted for making use of it and since I am a creature of the south, a feeling of light and space was of paramount importance to me. But, like a magician, Roger Banks-Pye made large spaces out of small ones, drew the light in from the east and the west, created a palette of color and an ambiance that were both English in atmosphere but also characteristically me. Now, even on dreary, rainy days, it feels sunny and bright here.

Perhaps you will think this is a designer's job after all, but don't forget that I too am a designer. My standards are exacting, my taste is particular, my requirements are precise, and only the most sensitive collaborator can be in tune with this. Roger understood my taste perfectly. He gave me my perfect English house—Valentino style.

Valentino

Valentino's green-and-white checks are used to line the walls, for the window dressing, and for the slipcovers, forming a perfect foil for the rich casings of the books (right).

a Blueprint
for living

*B*lue-and-white checked dishcloths at the window and a black floral chintz pasted onto the floorboards is an extraordinary way to furnish a room. Particularly so when this challenging scheme is found in the London townhouse apartment of a famous decorator from the distinguished firm of Colefax and Fowler, synonymous with traditional English decoration and chintz-filled interiors—and the chintz is from their archives. But Roger Banks-Pye is one of the most original decorators to emerge in Britain. At first glance his work might appear quite traditional because of the predominant use of antiques, old pictures, and accessories, but closer inspection reveals that in fact he is always re-inventing so that conventional elements can be revitalized and seen anew. For fifteen years he has cut a swathe through over-decorated drawing rooms—his interiors are instantly recognizable for their famously comfortable and friendly conversational air. To achieve this relaxed feel, he believes, a room needs pattern tempered with checks and solid colors, wooden tables at the right height with flowers on them, carefully positioned lamps

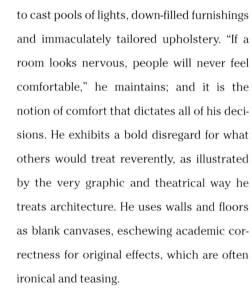

to cast pools of lights, down-filled furnishings and immaculately tailored upholstery. "If a room looks nervous, people will never feel comfortable," he maintains; and it is the notion of comfort that dictates all of his decisions. He exhibits a bold disregard for what others would treat reverently, as illustrated by the very graphic and theatrical way he treats architecture. He uses walls and floors as blank canvases, eschewing academic correctness for original effects, which are often ironical and teasing.

Working for Colefax and Fowler was a firm ambition for Roger Banks-Pye even when a student, but it was not until his 29th birthday in 1977 that his dream was realized. It was some time after joining the firm that his exceptional talent emerged. Unusually for a designer, he worked in the antiques department, an appointment that lasted two years. He then transferred to the decorating team of Stanley Falconer, where he began to learn the mechanics and grammar of decoration in the grand Colefax manner.

The backbone of Colefax and Fowler's business, first established by Sibyl Colefax and John Fowler in 1934, is the grand decoration of houses in the English countryside. When the aristocratic American society hostess Nancy Lancaster took over Sibyl's role after the Second World War and she joined John Fowler at 39 Brook Street W1 in 1957, the Colefax grand style became rather more relaxed under her influence: a combination of elegance and "cozy clutter".

Finding new ways to interpret the John Fowler/Nancy Lancaster style in very different settings, Roger Banks-Pye has developed an inspirational and highly idiosyncratic style. He is aware of the need to be a step or two ahead, not to slavishly copy and rehash old-fashioned techniques or "rust on Fowler's laurels," as he puts it. He believes that John Fowler would have moved on, and the couturier Sir Hardy Amies, a great admirer of Roger's work, agrees: "We both feel that if Fowler had been alive today he would have changed his style and made it more simple."

Nancy Lancaster always had what Sir Cecil Beaton referred to as a healthy disregard for the sanctity of important pieces. She put the ordinary and appealing beside the

Roger has filled his London drawing room with things that inspire him (left). Books, whether the latest literary biography or a beautifully illustrated monograph of an artist who interests him, are frequently consulted and so are piled up on his desk or stacked on chairs. Pictures stand ready, waiting to be placed. Nothing is ever static, and the display is constantly changing.

Quality and enormous elegance signify a Banks-Pye interior; crisp linen skirts Valentino's bathtub to temper the heavy masculinity of the room (right).

grand and imposing. The nearest modern equivalent to Nancy Lancaster, Roger Banks-Pye has a similar fear of pretension, but, like her, he observes the highest standards: tables in pools of lamplight, sparkling silver or brass, rooms scented with cut flowers and candles, bedside tables with water, a light, the telephone, a pencil and pad. In his own English country house, in Wiltshire, a large stone mullioned rectory with Gothic arches, he has preserved the established atmosphere and style but introduced comfort and

Sketching was Roger's constant occupation from a very early age, and it is a skill and passion that has served him very well in his career as an interior decorator. It has the practical advantage of enabling him to produce detailed drawings of room plans for his clients, absolutely to scale when necessary (below). His sketches are beautifully done and always suggest rooms full of life and warmth (opposite), rather than being flat, uninspiring floor plans. And having an artist's eye, being accustomed to looking at things properly in order to capture every detail, also affects the way in which he views things: the shape of objects, their relationships with each other, their space and position are always carefully thought out.

fun. This house is his testing ground: the place where he is able to experiment with ideas and techniques. When he first moved in he was fascinated by how the rooms had just grown, somehow evolved over the years around apple-green gloss walls and a great deal of furniture. It was living in and looking at this house that taught Roger the timeless appeal of effortless decoration.

But Roger's passion for decoration first manifested itself in his childhood home in Sheffield. He remembers painting the kitchen

with colors from 1950s paint charts, choosing navy blue for the fridge and for the washing machine. With his mother and sister he visited grand houses in the area such as Kedleston, Hardwick and Chatsworth, which as a young boy he thought were like fairytale castles. Art was an early inspiration, and he was never without paper and pencil. Attending the local grammar school, he spent most of the time in the art department. At nine he drew his first fashion collection, total copies of Christian Dior, a precocious demonstration of his brilliant eye for a mentor—Dior's New Look was easily the best to imitate. Drawing was a key factor in developing his eye. He always maintained that taking a photograph of some detail taught you next to nothing. "You have to be able to understand and remember clearly, especially when you need to re-use what has aroused your interest. I draw things that I can use again in decoration, like pavilions or finials."

At 18 he moved to London to study interior design at the North London Polytechnic. On Saturday mornings he would make a pilgrimage to Habitat, that temple of taste and style, as he recalls it, and on the way he looked through the windows of Belgravia houses to check how the draperies were tied back, stopping by at the bins outside the Colefax and Fowler showroom to collect swatches to use in his presentation boards at college. After four years he acquired an Honours degree, along with his tutor's disheartening observation that his capriciousness made him unsuited for a career in interior design and that the theater might be a more suitable choice.

"Whatever you do in your decorating philosophy, be brave. Have stark red walls if you wish. But never wish you hadn't taken your vision right to the end. Make a bold statement."

Post finals, after a period of unemployment, he was fortunate enough to spend time working for Ewan Macleod, a gifted architect specializing in the restoration and adaptation of traditional domestic-scale buildings. It was during this period that Roger learned the invaluable lesson that architecture relates to human scale. This fundamental truth gives his interiors their friendly familiarity. Nothing is imposing, impractical, or inconvenient.

Lodgings in a room in an empty shell of a house that was being renovated provided him with a canvas upon which to try out his early ideas on decoration. He glaze-painted the walls terracotta and stuffed the rooms full of furniture. Combing London antiques and junk shops also became part of his routine, one that has persisted to this day. He was never much interested in what was generally considered fine in antiques, his taste being for the strange—those odd pieces that 20 years ago most people passed over. Scale, form, pattern, and color were the essential qualities he looked for, and it was this graphic aspect of things that ultimately shaped his work. Portobello Road market, that treasure trove of wonderful discoveries, provided him with a Louis Philippe bed, and a marvelous old screen covered with moth-eaten fabric that gave his modest room great mystery and glamour. He learned that if the best was unaffordable, cramming a space with what he dismisses now as "rubbish—books, easels, screens, the lot" was all that was required to make it interesting. This experience fuelled his inclination towards decoration and, with a financial partner, Banks-Pye Designs was launched.

color," remembers Roger. Later he was invited to spend a weekend there. Feeling like Kingsley Amis' accident-prone antihero in *Lucky Jim*, he recalls staying up late into the night to sketch and, at about 2 a.m., going upstairs and being fascinated by a beige balloon shade hung with thick bullion fringe. Ever curious, he undid it to find out how it worked and the cords broke and clouds of dust erupted, so he had to stand on boxes to return it to its faded and dusty former self.

He learned from John Fowler the little luxuries that can cosset. "John Fowler had incredible knowledge and subtleties and I suspect he learned those touches of comfort from Nancy Lancaster, who was both charming and alarming. What I didn't realize then was his incredible attention to detail." Roger also shares with Fowler a taste for the modest. The *objet trouvé* and the off-the-shelf items of apparently little worth give him great pleasure, but they are always chosen for their clarity of design and the visual contribution they can make to a room. This contrasts sharply with some other interior decorators, who will opt for important and

Around 1970, Roger was invited through mutual friends to lunch at John Fowler's Hunting Lodge. He bought a new suit, and, for his host, a white azalea in a simple Suffolk rush basket. John Fowler impressed his young guest by immediately removing a cachepot with flowers mid-table and replacing it with Roger's gift. "The Hunting Lodge was magical—comfortable and stylish, filled with painted furniture, pots, baskets, column lamps, washed-out color, just thin layers of

A supreme love for fabric is the primary influence on the way Roger executes his window dressing treatments, which are always models of elegance (above).

The finish is all. *Roger would never sacrifice the whole for the sake of the final details. A floral border on the draperies, which echoes the delicate tracery of trailing flowers on the carpet, is itself bound by a thin line of solid pink (right). A deeper pink braid is applied to the edges of the wallpaper, along the architrave (far right) and below the cornice, giving the illusion of walls that are upholstered with fabric.*

This delightful sketch is filled with elements
that are typical of a Roger Banks-Pye interior.
Pattern is used throughout the room, picked up in
the slipcovers, in the drapery fabric and as a single
motif on the cushions. The picture is selected for its
subject matter and its place in the scheme. A screen
is added for vertical emphasis, and a table,
conveniently placed near the chair, provides a
surface on which to display an elegant piece of
topiary. Roger's beloved checks cover the walls. All
these elements are skillfully executed in just a few
lines with a simple color wash to suggest
textures and colors.

rare artefacts, coupled with the finest-quality
materials, to lend authority to their work.

Roger's supreme skill is in handling fabric,
and he has taught himself through his
absolute passion for material, which he uses
in the closest way a decorator has come to
being a couturier. Nobody since John Fowler
in his heyday has approached this aspect of
decorating with such confidence. It is hardly
surprising that both Sir Hardy Amies and
Valentino became devotees of his work. Their

"*Every job has the same requirements: to look good, to be comfortable, and to work as a whole, although the priorities move about. I'm rather like a cook making a basic cake but adding a bit of ginger to perk it up.*"

rigorous standards and pursuit of perfection enable them both to appreciate the efforts that Roger makes on their behalf.

At Colefax and Fowler, Stanley Falconer was a great influence, not just on taste but in teaching Roger how to tackle commissions and how to get the work completed on time, maintaining the quality of work for which the firm is renowned. But the opportunity that really enabled him to develop his style was the promotional aspect of the firm's work. This covered designing and decorating the window displays for the showrooms. He also styled the promotional photography and

Whether producing a classical window treatment (above) or experimenting with fresh ideas, Roger is equally confident. The sketches shown here are typical of his imaginative approach: exploring the theme of buttons and buttonholes, he devised a valance inspired by shirt cuffs, with variations on the shape (below). Buttons are used as a closing device down the edges of the drapery panels and to attach fabric to the walls.

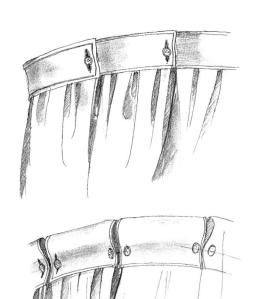

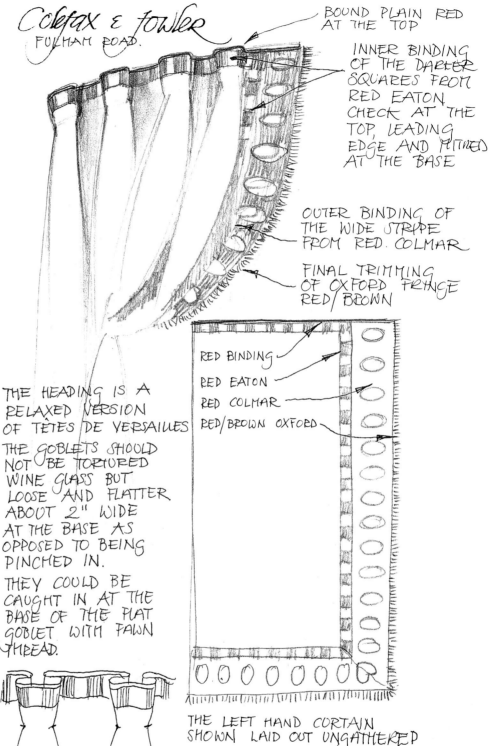

Colefax & Fowler
FULHAM ROAD.

BOUND PLAIN RED AT THE TOP

INNER BINDING OF THE DARKER SQUARES FROM RED EATON CHECK AT THE TOP, LEADING EDGE AND MITRED AT THE BASE

OUTER BINDING OF THE WIDE STRIPE FROM RED. COLMAR

FINAL TRIMMING OF OXFORD FRINGE RED/BROWN

THE HEADING IS A RELAXED VERSION OF TÊTES DE VERSAILLES

THE GOBLETS SHOULD NOT BE TORTURED WINE GLASS BUT LOOSE AND FLATTER ABOUT 2" WIDE AT THE BASE AS OPPOSED TO BEING PINCHED IN.

THEY COULD BE CAUGHT IN AT THE BASE OF THE FLAT GOBLET WITH FAWN THREAD.

RED BINDING
RED EATON
RED COLMAR
RED/BROWN OXFORD

THE LEFT HAND CURTAIN SHOWN LAID OUT UNGATHERED

decorated stands for shows such as Decorex, the home furnishings and fabric trade fair.

In 1989 Colefax and Fowler took over the Jane Churchill fabric company, which is today headed by Ann Grafton, launching a wide selection of checks, stripes, solids, and bright motifs. It presented Roger with a new range to work with, and he uses it frequently for children's rooms, linings, and cushions. "Ann Grafton's Jane Churchill has given another aspect to the Colefax group—we're more serious but what I love about Churchill fabrics is that they are fun and light-hearted, not frighteningly traditionalist."

The style and proportion of the window are crucial factors in helping Roger decide how he is going to dress it. The overall shape will dictate whether he will opt for a single pair of draperies, with perhaps a stationary panel or a pull-down shade as an extra embellishment, or treat each portion of the window separately, as left.

Nothing is left to chance when Roger draws up a design. He knows exactly what is needed to achieve the result he wants, and technical details, including the colors, fabrics, measurements, method of construction, and even the thread, are always specified to an exact degree, as these plans for a pair of draperies for a window display demonstrate.

No object is so humble that it should not be given a decorative treatment. A matchbox, for example, would be used and discarded by most people. But Roger will take the time to paint on something that, as a smoker, he uses and looks at constantly.

It was Roger's window displays in particular that became a talking point. Their flair and spontaneity were sufficiently outstanding to attract acclaim. This success encouraged him. He experimented with the detail of draperies, upholstery, trimmings, and a wide use of accessories. In dressing the windows he sometimes used the cheapest of props, such as painted picket fencing, garden baskets planted with moss and bulbs, charmingly elaborate slipcovers over the backs of tatty iron garden furniture. He is never satisfied with doing anything standard or repeating himself. Using his consummate skills as a set designer—but one who is concerned with the perfect finish to a job rather than the superficial effect most set designers aim for—he built up a grammar of designing draperies and upholstery that he has applied to his work ever since. It is his ability to evoke atmosphere within the confines of a small window space, coupled with a meticulous eye for detail, that fascinated all who saw them. Lady Boothby, a friend, recalls one particular design that attracted her attention: "I walked past the Colefax and Fowler shop on the Fulham Road, and this window done up in blue and white and yellow stopped me in my tracks, it was so inviting. His windows beckon you to come into the shop. On those London winter nights when it is so cheerless and dank and cold, his windows are warm and inviting, a splash of light and color."

Working as an interior decorator, he has built up his own team within the company, with his own schemes and houses. He develops strong relationships with his clients—probably closer than most decorators. With his warm personality, love of gossip, and sometimes outrageous sense of humor, he endears people to him, and he is very accommodating to clients' needs and ideas. All his friends have been recipients of his caustic humor, and of all the descriptions of his temperament that he relishes, sardonic is his favorite. Seldom without a cigarette, bored by food, he throws a warm, appreciative wrap around the lives of his friends. Lyn Rothman, originally a client, describes how he does this: "We became the closest of friends about ten years ago and at about that time he started sending me regular postcards and letters. I have them all in a book. They are extremely funny and clever, and always arrived at a time when he knew I needed a good

Roger's love for blue and white, especially checks, manifests itself in his choice of furnishing fabrics (below left), the ornamental objects he surrounds himself with (right) and even his clothes and household linens (above).

laugh. What touches me most is the time and trouble he takes to find just the right cards and precisely the right wording—such genius." The designer William Yeoward believes that this generosity of spirit influences Roger's designs: "His style has ease and humour, never being serious or contrived."

A certain sense of morality can be detected behind Roger Banks-Pye's creativity, so that his interiors achieve a purer beauty which does not rely on a deep pocket. In his own very subtle way he can circumvent the world of social pretension and material excess. He is able to introduce his highly individual style of interior design to people who went to Colefax and Fowler for the "Establishment" look, and who ended up with a fresh interpretation of that look. Bridget Glasgow, who was his design assistant at Colefax for six years, says that "he never gets stuck on one idea and I don't believe the firm would have progressed with such confidence without his influence."

"One becomes bored supplying the same solutions to the same problems: I need to be constantly amused, and it intrigues me to discover and use different approaches."

Scale and Proportion

Architectural
Detailing

𝒲orking for architects, actually gutting houses, taught Roger Banks-Pye how the internal structure of buildings relates to human scale. For example, why is a door measurement standard worldwide? Because it takes the height of a man, the breadth of the shoulders and has a mid-rail at waist level to support the handles and locks. Roger is fascinated by this sort of detail, and the historical influence human habitation has had upon houses. His first consideration in a room is always whether the overall shape works: the height of the ceiling, the proportions, the focal point. If it does not, he will always consider ways of remedying it without resorting to major structural changes, such as designing a fire-place facing, adding architectural details like dadoes and paneling, or simply changing the doors. Then he applies decoration to camouflage any disadvantages with color and pattern.

These techniques are especially important in those awkward spaces that no one spends a great deal of time in, such as entrance halls, stairways, and landings. When he was invited to decorate the home of the chairman of Colefax and Fowler, David Green, and his wife

This entrance hall was remodeled to introduce symmetry and architectural fluency, with its limed oak staircase and graphically segmented paved floor (left). The defined proportions are balanced with a large oak chest and a dark-framed contemporary painting. The door to the guest lavatory is concealed within the hall paneling (above).

The area formed by the square bay on the half landing is not wasted: an Indo-Portuguese settee is flanked by narrow Regency giltwood mirrors.

Judy, the first thing he considered in the turn-of-the-century house was the lofty entrance hall with its coffered ceiling. The architecture of the house was influenced by the Arts and Crafts movement, and the imposing hall, with its huge square flagstones has walls gessoed in pale chalky beige, with limed oak stairs and banisters. Originally, it had a single asymmetrical beam running across the ceiling to the right. This imbalance offended Roger's eye so he added a second beam on the left-hand side, a relatively simple way to remedy the visual imperfection.

Staircases can be difficult architectural features to handle well, but they are never overlooked in Roger's decorating schemes. Indeed, he has firm views about their treatment. In the Greens' house the stairs are carpeted in a Brussels weave, bordered in beige and brown, leading up to and beyond the half-landing, where leaded windows are framed by duck-egg and cappuccino curtains, their blue frayed edges matched by the blue of an Indo-Portuguese bench seat. Roger nearly always carpets stair treads with a heavy-duty overall pattern, anchored with brass rods, and lets that patterned carpet determine his choice of color for the banisters and handrail: "I hate white balusters. Lots of sticks painted white look like a blind man's convention." Roger favors painting them cream or, even better, a dark color to make them disappear. If the stair carpet is blue he will paint the banisters blue to match, with the handrail in polished mahogany. For one particularly ornate scheme the stair rods are painted to simulate bronze. Landings are important oases on the ascent, whether the

The tall stairway window affords enough light to allow the shapely Italian-strung draperies to partially obscure it and soften the lines (above). A curved dado rail mirrors the handrail. Roger thinks dark-painted stair spindles far more chic than white and here has painted them the cobalt blue of the carpet.

A hallway gives the opportunity to set the theme of the house as one enters (right). Here tall elegance is accentuated by the narrow faux *marble* panels and the luxuriant cascade of the valance's cascades. Sisal flooring adds informality and the warm mustard, beige, and cream colors unite the whole scheme.

narrow windowed stair landing of the narrow town house or the Greens' more generously apportioned landing, which forms an inviting suntrap. These spaces without inhabitants are there just to be admired, so permit bolder stylish excesses than elsewhere in the house. They provide a scope for little theatrical set pieces, even something as simple as a stationary drapery panel, a shade, and a candelabra. An over-scaled window treatment Roger designed for the anteroom to Nancy Lancaster's Yellow Room at 39 Brook Street, London, for example—"a little harmless excess" in draperies, as he describes it—works in a space where nobody spends more than a minute. The anteroom is irregular, dark, and awkward and has eight doors. Known as the Painted Landing, it was originally decorated over 40 years ago by John Fowler and Nancy Lancaster. There were no draperies, just a mirror-faced shutter which slides open into the wall depth. Roger dressed the window for an American decoration magazine, dressing this shuttered space with a single asymmetrical panel, neoclassically draped. He admits that he has dramatized the space in a way that would be inappropriately excessive were the space inhabited.

In larger rooms such one-off, isolated treatments will not work because there are different architectural considerations. Many of the houses that Roger has worked on, for example, have the common difficulty of a typical English townhouse; the double drawing room with a folding door or arch in the middle, a fireplace on either side of the room division, and pairs of windows at either end, making the furniture placement difficult. In Valentino's London residence the library and the adjoining drawing room are identically sized, each with a central fireplace. In order to link the two rooms Roger took the Valentino green-and-white checks and used them as a common factor. On one side he built bookshelves, which he painted green then gilded. The walls were upholstered in green checked silk, which was also used to dress the window. The same fabric was then used as a linking factor for the accessories in the drawing room, which is predominantly green tempered with a floral pattern in crimson and yellow.

The inevitability of visual division created by an archway between the two parts of Valentino's drawing room (left) has been turned to an advantage, so that each area may have its own decorative flavor, while a sense of continuity and balance is maintained through the addition of magnificent Regency mirrors above the twin fireplaces.

Changing the
Focus

Proportion is the geometry of space, which can be measured in inches or else perceived by the eye alone. The decorator's real skill is to transform a small space, manipulating it with color and pattern so that architectural details appear larger, or selecting and arranging furniture to alter the focus in a room. Roger believes that changing the scale in a small space can be as simple as exaggerating the vertical—always the vertical—with full-height doors, floor to ceiling; tall pictures; urns and china on brackets; a big armoire with pots on top; anything to take the eye up so it does not roam around the box-like proportions. Disguise, and what he calls "trickery" to emphasize the vertical, can be as simple as hanging pictures over doors.

In a second-floor studio flat in Chelsea, owned by Trudi Ballard, head of public relations, press, and advertising at Colefax and Fowler, a windowless bathroom was sandwiched between two rooms, one large and one very much smaller. Originally, the big room was used as a kitchen-dining room with living space, and the little room at the back served as the bedroom, but Roger took a fresh look at the way the way the space had been allocated for different functions and decided to

***Promoting a sense of space and flexibility of use** in this studio apartment meant relocating the kitchen into what used to be the bedroom (above), adding a huge but simply constructed wardrobe (left) and designing a day bed that turns into a double bed (right). Vertical emphasis is given by using every inch of space to the ceiling and elegant chandeliers to draw the eye upward. A monochrome decorative palette and simple, elegant draperies and soft furnishings increase the sense of spaciousness and light.*

make the smaller room the kitchen. Banking the oven, sink, and fridge into rustic cupboards with a single open display shelving unit, he left space in front of the sash window to squeeze in a tiny table and four chairs for entertaining. In the drawing room he removed the kitchen, that stood behind a bi-fold louvered door, and installed a huge cabinet 24 inches deep, where the kitchen had stood. "After buying this flat in a fashionable area of London there was very little money left for decoration," explains Roger. "I designed a wardrobe and we put it together—it cost little and has more impact and effect than an antique armoire." This handsome break-front wardrobe is made from inexpensive unplaned wood which has been whitewashed. "Kashmir Leaf" fabric by Jane Churchill is tacked in the panels of the doors. As a central focus to the room Roger designed a sofa that had to double as a bed. He added scroll arms at both ends of an ordinary twin bed so that four people can perch on it, two by two on each side. It is an elegant solution to a common problem. As Roger explains, "This flat is light-colored, light-pocketed, and light-hearted."

Architects deliberately place low-ceilinged lobbies and entrance halls leading to higher-ceilinged rooms to maximize the experience of the space stretching beyond. To imitate this visual deception, Roger lined the walls of the tiny entrance hall leading to Trudi's apartment in butterscotch-colored checks to frame the bigger monochrome room beyond. This exaggerated change in scale takes the eye upward. Understanding space is the first step toward transforming and using it. High ceilings and the neutral color make the room "breathe easily", as Roger describes it, and he emphasizes that height further by stretching the vertical scale to its upmost: the cabinet, nearly 10 feet tall on a plinth, has inexpensive creamware pots and baskets piled on top of it. Shelves on one side of the fireplace, and vertical stacks of pictures and mirrors on the walls all underline the height.

In a featureless room that lacks an obvious focal point, such as a fireplace or a big picture window, Roger will always allocate a piece of furniture to fulfill that function. Here an early-19th-century Russian mahogany desk, deliberately vastly overscaled for the size of the room, performs that role (right). The placing of the rest of the furniture in the room revolves around the desk. The style and design of the desk, with its three separate tall top cabinets, was chosen for the height it gives to the room, and this was further emphasized by adding a pair of urns on either side and a large vase at the very top in a beautifully balanced tapering arrangement.

"There seems to be only one stock molding for dado rails that everyone uses. It costs a little more to run off a simple classic molding, but it's like having a good leather belt. Quality will always show."

Rooms without architectural details present another kind of challenge. No focal point like a fireplace in a boring room? Take the eye upward with a huge armoire or a boldly striped wallpaper set above the chair rail. Awkward windows? No point in framing them with swags and cascades. Rather block them with a shade and then frame them with a fabric that takes the eye in from the window.

A striped wallpaper was especially designed to add vertical emphasis to this low-ceilinged room, and a dado added since there was no existing architectural detailing (above left). A gilded wooden fillet runs along the top for a special finish.

To break up the flat run of pictures on the wall with three-dimensional objects, brackets were added on which mirror-black vases are displayed (above), reflecting the urns displayed on the desk opposite. Adding brackets is a visual technique Roger often uses to direct attention upward.

Roger has decorated an apartment which presented just these challenges. Designed for an American businessman who divides his time between London and New York, it illustrates the ability of a skillful decorator to change scale by adding architectural details, then camouflage ugly proportions with pattern and color. Comprising two rooms, a bathroom, and a cell-like kitchen, this 1930s

flat had been blandly decorated as a show flat. Roger reports on the scheme he devised: "It was a concrete box with no architectural detailing at all. The first thing I did was disguise the cheap, featureless doors leading from the entrance hall with double-paneled ones, and then I added new architraves. There was no dado rail, so I put in one painted in three shades of broken white and added a

Tartan-covered armchairs drawn up to a round mahogany Russian table form a secondary furniture grouping in one corner for a variation in height levels (above). The black marble-topped table can be drawn into the center of the room to double as a dining table. The decorative objects in the room, such as the table lamp base, the shade on the brass floor lamp, and the frames on the animal prints on the walls, are predominantly black to act as a strong foil to the rich red and highly patterned furnishings, carpet and draperies.

gilt fillet to give it glitter and glamour." The wallpaper above the dado, "Chesterfield Stripe", inspired by a 19th-century design, was especially printed in red and brown on cream colors to visually raise the ceiling with bold vertical bands. Like the doors, the cornice is in three shades of white and beneath it a gilt wooden fillet. Finding a focal point in a box-like room with no fireplace and no central feature is important. "I wanted something imposing since there was no view, only one dark window. So I bought overscaled furniture, like the enormous Russian Empire mahogany escritoire which is very handsome. It brought to a boring modest little wall a certain focal point. On either side I hung pairs of curious animal prints: camels, dromedaries, and elephants."

Roger believes that in small spaces, the bigger the pattern the better. The living room, although it is the biggest room in the place, is in reality only 15 feet square. So he made it look very bold, modeled on the comfortable lines of a gentleman's club. The Russian desk and a vastly proportioned red velvet sofa, a richly patterned Turkish carpet teamed with a fabric covered in sprawling tree poppies for draperies and armchairs, certainly exaggerated the scale. "Don't be afraid in small rooms to use bold pattern and intense color. The mistake so many people make is to think a small room needs delicate treatment. The cozy atmosphere I wanted to create relied on using furnishings and furniture that are overscaled in this way."

In a small apartment it is important not to give what Roger describes as "visual indigestion" by changing pattern or color from room to room, but rather to distribute the basic scheme throughout to give a uniform feel. In the bedroom Colefax and Fowler "Tree Poppy" linen appears once again, not only at the windows but also battened to the walls and doors and across the flat fronts of the wardrobe doors so that the wardrobe filling one wall of the small room disappears. Even the wardrobe doorknobs are painted with

poppies and leaves in a *trompe l'oeil* effect so that the line is uninterrupted. A slender parson's table, designed by Roger and set in the corner of the room to act as a bedside table, is also covered with the patterned linen to lose it against the background, leaving the emphasis on the blonde wood Charles X furniture distributed around the rest of the room.

Conversely, given the space of a big room to play with, Roger will readily mix different patterns and colors on upholstered furniture in order to add dynamism. By changing patterns in different-scaled chintzes in the Greens' sitting room, and teaming them with solids in palest coral, cream, and brown, and contrast fabric in checks, he controlled the different seating groups in the room, adding a sense of movement to occupy the spaces. "Always scale up, not down. Everyone is terrified of making things too big—if in doubt make it bigger, not smaller. Instead of spindly chairs, say, it is more generous to have a big wing chair in old leather. Much too big will always be better than too small."

Whereas most designers would use small-scale subtle detailing in a small space, Roger takes the view that there is no reason why bold pattern should not be used in a broad, confident sweep. In the bedroom (right) he has continued the same patterns that were used in the drawing room. The fabric used for the soft furnishings in the first room is here used to cover the walls and at the window, and the same Brussels weave carpet is used on the floor. A further dimension is added by the use of a sprigged motif weave for the wing chair, the bed skirt and the headboard. In place of a fireplace, a desk is once again used as a focal point. A mirror hung above it serves a decorative function rather than a practical one: too high for normal use, it reflects the clock and figures placed before it.

To marry with the design of the carpet the flat of the baseboard is heavily stippled dark green. A tabby-braid trimming, specially dyed to match the printed linen upholstered on the walls, finishes the edge to prevent the fabric fraying (opposite).

To camouflage the built-in wardrobes that line one wall of the bedroom, the flat-fronted doors were covered with the same patterned linen that lines the walls. The door handles were painted by hand in a trompe l'oeil design so that the line of the pattern is uninterrupted (left). For a neat finish the whole of the interior is lined with a fern-patterned paper (below).

dado into rooms. It should relate to the waist on the human body while the baseboard relates to the feet." Roger never paints the baseboard white, always off-black or the darkest tone of the wall or floor color. Lyn Rothman, a client and friend, remembers his attention to detail when he was working on her home: "He is a complete perfectionist in every respect, from the way he dresses to the exact positioning of each piece of furniture in a room—two inches off and the look is lost!"

In an attempt to make rooms more classical people often fit elaborate but underscaled cornices. Roger's rule is to keep the molding simple, but, as always, his advice is to scale up rather than down, and to pick out the plasterwork in three shades of the same color. If there is no existing cornice, and it is not a practical proposition to add one, Roger will come up with other solutions to frame the room. In a child's bedroom, for example, he cut a narrow border of squares from a checked fabric, backed it with paper, and glued it to the wall beneath the ceiling and around the doors. It is very modest solution but it defines the proportions of the room.

The other architectural feature Roger will consider is a dado rail or chair rail, and whatever the height of a room, he is insistent that the dado rail height should not vary from standing 33 inches above floor level. "People think they can make a room appear more Georgian if they fiddle with the height of the dado, but believe me, that is the correct proportion, whatever the size of the room. Victorian staircases used to have a high dado, but the mistake made now is to put that high

The Course of
Color

Blue and White

Roger's attitude toward design, fabric, and color is to constantly seek to be innovative and amusing; he has no desire to emulate the entirely traditional approach of many decorators, whose tendency is to create purely period settings. Rather, he promotes a gentle evolution of 20th-century decoration, to broaden the boundaries of the accepted "classic" look and give his interiors a fresh twist and wider palette. However, he would not dream of compromising his high standards of decorative integrity and exquisite finish by so much as a fraction for the sake of some quirky modernism: whatever element he employs to surprise and excite it will never be detrimental to the harmony of the finished scheme.

A bold and exciting use of color is evident throughout his interiors. In particular—above all other single colors or color combinations—blue and white are pivotal in many of his designs. Indeed, he happily admits to a passion that borders on fanaticism, and uses any opportunity he can to introduce it. There are several reasons for his enthusiasm for this particular combination. Primarily, he feels that this versatile pairing can be used to great effect in virtually any situation, however grand or diminutive the scheme. If a crisp and contemporary look is

__Blue-and-white "things that amuse"__ massed together in Roger's London kitchen (left) include painted vegetable boxes and an abundance of china, from tea caddies to bright café mugs (above and right), making a fresh collection. Scraps of fabric and even rolls of plastic provide inspiration while they await incorporation in one of his designs. "Nothing stays more than a month!" he says.

sought, then the paler blues such as sapphire and cobalt are the ones to use, smartened and structured with a hint of black here and there perhaps. If the room is south-facing and full of light, then a cool gray-blue will work, but beware of dull northern light which will kill most blues, except perhaps a red-biased blue. Also keep in mind that blue dyes are

In Valentino's kitchen conservatory, blue-and-white fabrics are used for the sophisticated check of the ingenious overhead gathered shades, for the cushion pads and the halfcovers slipped over the backs of the chairs, and in a pretty Provençal-style tablecloth. French and Chinese porcelain plates, some of which are actually sunk into the plaster of the yellow-painted walls for a permanent mosaic effect, contribute to the international feeling of the room.

unstable and will fade quicker than other colors, especially when placed in direct light. Blue and white will work either as a solitary statement or put together in a glorious multitude of materials, paintwork, paper, and artefacts to combine many blues of different patterns and textures. Roger's seasoned advice when dealing with multiple shades of

blue is that there is a danger of disastrous clashes only when just two conflicting blues are used in juxtaposition. Add a third, fourth, fifth—however many the scale and economics of the piece will stand—and the whole will come together in a delicious melting pot. The kitchen, appropriately, is probably the room with the most potential for exploiting this

Throwing in a touch of gilt will add an extra fillip to a blue-and-white scheme. Bells of Ireland (Moluccella laevis) tumbling over the top of a willow-patterned urn (below right) supply a further sharp contrast in a splash of brilliant green. The joy of using blue and white is that they form such an accessible combination and look good in any room situation, whether formal or informal, as in the napkins and the tablecloth in the tea-time setting below.

bold application. At its most informal and eclectic, materials, ornaments, and artefacts with a broad provenance can be introduced in as informal a collaboration as you like—there is no room for a timid hand when the blue-and-white saturation look is sought. The idea is to put together all manner of patterned fabrics—checks, chintzes, toiles,

spots, stripes—and use them for shades, slipcovers, cushions, napkins, tablecloths, and curtains. Scraps could be framed instead of pictures, dish towels may be wrapped around ceiling light cords by way of disguise or draped, handkerchief-style, to transform a boring lampshade. If you can't find enough blue-and-white china to fill the shelves, paint cardboard vegetable cartons begged from the neighbourhood grocer in blue-and-white stripes and stuff rustic baskets with painted angular twigs and blown eggs and pine cones to fill the spaces and add a different emphasis in shape and texture. Delft-style tiles and Indian cotton rugs would complement each other on the vertical and horizontal planes.

Perhaps one of Roger's most fulsome experiments in blue-and-white decoration has been the treatment of some of his own rooms, both in London and in his house in the country. His kitchen, for example, has evolved its blue-and-white persona over many years since its inception, long before every glossy magazine extolled the virtues of this look—not least, perhaps, because it is so seductively photogenic! Now the simple dresser frames a massed display of china, cans, and pretty bits of junk. However, the arrangement is crucial to the look, and Roger takes great care to achieve a sense of order and balance. The result is an eclectic, inexpensive *mise-en-scène* that shifts and evolves because it is artistic, functional, and fun.

Naturally, a high level of sophistication and perfect finishing was a prerequisite in the couturier Valentino's London house. His kitchen, therefore, is a fine example of a smart, restrained, and discerning use of blue

"I've always liked blue-and-white china and suddenly, I just discovered blue-and-white checks and became impassioned of them. Someone once told me they are the only thing that is tidy and logical about my mind."

and white. Here, a large-scale checked cotton is gathered into draw shades over the sloping windows and the back and seat cushions of the wicker chairs. A Provençal-style table-cloth and a display of fine French and Chinese porcelain complete the picture. There is no clutter, no fuss.

The magic of blue-and-white fabric lies in its transglobal character, whether it is home-spun or sophisticated, classic or modern. In his own homes, Roger exploits all these attributes. A handmade patchwork throw lies alongside flamboyant leopard prints and smart stripes; his bed is made up with a crisp assortment of multi-checked cottons; and his bathroom is a two-toned tapestry with a sheer gingham shade and bath curtains and a frayed patchwork checkerboard wall.

Blue and white will look spectacularly handsome wherever you put them, whatever the lighting conditions and atmosphere of their given location. Perhaps the "signature" that is most likely to reveal Roger's hand in a decorative scheme is his frequent use of blue and white as a counterpoint to highly decorated rooms and richly colored and patterned chintzes. The effect is superb in its simplest form: adding a single, deeply comfortable chair beautifully tailored in a blue-and-white check, for example, is like providing iced mineral water in a crystal glass during a rich meal.

***Homely or sophisticated in turn**, blue and white makes an adaptable team. Roger paints objects of all sorts to add to his ever-changing blue-and-white paraphernalia, even an original basket for a pot of cress (left). Different checks mixed together look really smart, as seen here on two beautifully tailored chairs (right).*

Yellow and Blue

Yellow and blue set each other off in a convivial way that is unique to this color duo. It probably has a lot to do with the psychological feel-good effect that they have on the viewer. Thoughts of spring flowers and fresh blue skies after a long gray winter, perhaps. Or an association with Mediterranean island colors. Whatever an individual's subconscious reaction, the point is that this pairing is easy on the eye and has a vast color range with which to play.

However, Roger would not use blue and yellow in the same way that he adopts blue and white with such a broad sweep. His supremely confident totally blue-and-white designs work because of the particular decorative and color grammar involved, which is very different when blue and yellow come together. The former can be used in a collective, free-handed manner because any number of blues, when balanced by white, will gel together in happy companionship. This is because there is no conflict when white of any tone is blue's companion. Yellow and blue together are technically trickier partners and need handling in a different way. When placed in juxtaposition they should be of equal color saturation, or one will kill the other—and probably deeply off end the viewer's eye. This is of prime concern when the yellow-blue combination to be used is an intense and dominant one, and all other decorative artefacts, materials, and colors in the room are of equal tonal density and weight.

In Roger's hands, yellow and blue together are used with a lightness of touch and sensitive discretion that entirely suits the sort of glamorous, comforting interiors he puts together. For example, he seldom

When yellow and blue are used together in a decorative scheme, their tonal balance and distribution within the room is of prime importance. Here they are used as a strong visual link between an interconnecting study and living room, while each part retains its own identity. The solid blue armchair in the yellow room is a dominant echo of the stong blue walls beyond.

Fowler showrooms when he was hunting down things to use in his celebrated window displays. The company's supreme specialist painter, George Oakes, had painted the canvas screen yellow with blue-and-white platters and plates all over it. The screen has been with Roger ever since, and he has used the blue/white/yellow device to great effect and amusement in several situations, not least in Valentino's conservatory kitchen, where a yellow wall is adorned with blue-and-

white dishes actually sunk into the fabric of the wall. The aura created in this lovely room is a sort of Mediterranean-meets-Chinese in an English environment.

When the colors used are as dominant as the blue used here, the furnishings need to be equally strong to act as a counterbalance. In this room that balance is provided by the strong yellow-brown of the *faux wood effect on the bookcases and the chunky outlines of the furniture. Off-whites and carefully selected flowers* (Viburnum opulus) *provide a mellow contrast.*

uses a yellow-and-blue fabric as the predominant theme in a room, preferring to separate the colors into different components and use them that way. He has used this scheme in the double drawing room of a town house. In the study half, the walls are a rich dark blue and, at the drawing room end, a glowing yellow. These colors are picked out in reverse in elements of fabric, paint, and decorative details which hold the two parts together without loss of individual identity. There are blue-and-white patterned chair covers in the "yellow" half but the bookshelves are painted yellowish *faux* bird's-eye maplewood in the "blue" portion. Yellow and blue are then included in small details such as in the cushions or in a hint of yellow on a decorative porcelain plate. In this way the wall color is not isolated from the room contents and a visual rhythm is maintained. The principal colors are complemented by the presence of the broken white architectural paintwork and the buff-colored sisal flooring.

Roger's enthusiasm for blue and yellow was fired when he discovered an old screen in the basement of one of the Colefax and

Yellow

Yellow can be a difficult surface color to introduce. Many yellows are too green and sharp, and Roger prefers to work with more mellow tones: creamy shades of primrose, amber, and straw, rather than harsh citrus shades and lurid canary colors. Sometimes just a glimpse of yellow is all that is needed in an interior to bring it to life: the lengthy hall corridor in a Scottish lodge ended with a white matte-painted wall at the kitchen entrance. Painting it yellow gloss ensures that when the door is open, the strong golden color illuminates the walls, which have been covered in a blue-and-white checkerboard design.

Whatever the medium used, surface color is usually applied in layers to give it depth. Paint, for example, may be mixed with glaze, sponged, dragged, or rolled to create different textured or tonal effects, which can be further improved by applying the color in several layers, with the paler tones allowed to show through. It is the phenomenon known in art terms as "pentimento". Paint colors are applied without a special finish only if the walls are already textured. This was the case in a sunny dining room, where the owners wanted an effect similar to that

created by the French Impressionist artist Claude Monet in his house at Giverney, north of Paris. The existing burlap walls were painted with white latex paint and sandpapered. The final coats were of a glorious butter-yellow paint, against which was set a collection of egg lithographs and a collection of blue-and-white china—as Monet had done at Giverney. Simple ladder-backed kitchen chairs are lined up against the walls as a decorative device. They too are painted yellow, but with subtle detailing: the crossbars are painted a paler lemon than the deeper yellow frame. And, as if to give her wholehearted support to the spirit of the project, the owner of the house then painted her mahogany dining table lemon to match.

One of Roger's greatest inspirations when it comes to using yellow is Nancy Lancaster's salon at the back of the Colefax and Fowler Brook Street premises, the famous yellow room, which is a showroom today. Marbled cornices and baseboards frame finely stippled and lacquered yellow walls. The view of the courtyard and its white flowering catalpa tree is framed in Italian-strung draperies of unlined yellow silk taffeta, caught at the head by bows from which hang two-toned ropes and tassels in bronze umber and yellow. Mirrors set in two blind arches around

Burlap covered walls sanded to a subtly flecked surface (left and above) provided the perfect textured background in this sunny dining room for several coats of rich buttery yellow paint.

With typical attention to detail, Roger painted the crossbars of the slipcovered farmhouse chairs in a contrasting paler yellow than the uprights (right). The owner then painted her antique mahogany table yellow to match—a bold move that astonished even Roger.

the door and into the architraves at each end of the room, give the illusion that the space is vast. Renowned for its mix of old and new, comfort and color, the room manages to be understated and at the same time extravagant, typical of the Colefax and Fowler charm. In his own Mayfair apartment, Roger wanted to re-create the atmosphere of hot Venice evenings, with their golden yellow glow. He did this by boiling up rabbit skin and pigments to make gesso, which he applied layer upon layer until he got the desired effect.

Colors change according to the surroundings. If you put a yellow square in a white frame it appears smaller than an identical yellow square inside a black frame. Tone also changes, so that yellow will appear lemony surrounded by white, but hot and vibrant on a black background. This can be put to the test in rooms: the yellow accents in this sunny London drawing room are soft. The walls are covered in a wheat-colored glaze, while a Colefax and Fowler chintz of a hydrangea design sets the colors for accents distributed around the room, with a green velvet sofa and chair upholstered in straw-colored ticking. The draperies have swagged bows, and a specially woven border of yellow and cream fringe—a shade that Roger so evocatively calls "old bones."

The spacious feel of this charming drawing room is enhanced by the wheat-colored glazed walls (right). The simple and elegant window treatment keeps the whole feeling of the room light and makes a mellow background to the comfortable furniture.

Delicate architectural detailing is picked out in Roger's signature style of using three closely shaded colors (above).

$\mathcal{G}reen$

Roger Banks-Pye's enthusiasm for blue and white, and its fortunate tonal sympathy with yellow, has meant that he has used green rather less often—green is not an easy color to mix with those particular shades. But the glory of green is that it is one of the easiest of colors to mix with itself: you can put any number of greens together and be confident that they will work. To see this principle borne out, just look to the country nature will throw acid lime with glaucous green, dark olive with rich emerald, and they will meld into one glorious whole.

Green has been the inspiration behind a number of interiors Roger has designed—one, appropriately enough, in the home of David Green, the chairman of Colefax and Fowler. This visual pun was the starting point for the color scheme that unites the master bedroom with an adjoining dressing room and bathroom, a charmingly fresh combination of greens and whites. The bedroom is covered in rich pattern. The fabric-lined walls are upholstered in panels of leafy roses on a white background, while pale green leaves twine across a mossy gray-green ground on the wall-to-wall carpet. This potentially overpowering mix of designs is kept in check by the use of closely shaded and toned hues, so that the overall effect is in fact muted and very smart. An adroit balance

Ever willing to impart his insights, John Fowler once told Roger, "All greens go together, child, just look at the hedgerows." Roger takes heed of that advice when putting together this nature-inspired scheme. A narrow tabby braid (above) outlines the architraves and conceals the tacks used to secure the fabric on the upholstered walls.

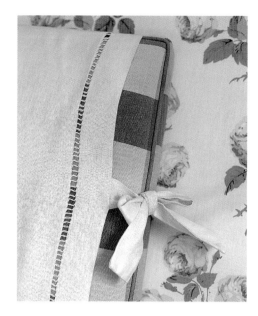

Crisply tied linen tapes secure the ivory linen slipcover to the headboard. The edges have been finished in an openwork hemstitch, echoing the graphic print of the check.

is kept throughout—to prevent the room from becoming too overtly feminine the floral walls are bordered by architraves, skirting boards and cornices painted in three shades of green. Checks distributed throughout the three rooms—as drapery linings, on the headboard, on the back of a chair—act as a counterpoint to the exuberant riot of

Limiting the palette to shades of green and white controls and calms the riot of pattern that has been used throughout the three adjoining rooms. The eight-paneled doors have been picked out in the same detailing as the architraves and cornice.

For a uniform finish all of the draperies and shades in the house are lined with a pale fawn cotton check. The draperies in the bedroom (above left) are edged with a natural looped wool fringe.

pattern, while expanses of white, as a background color and on the bed dressings, help to create a calm, cool, and very pretty oasis.

Green was an obvious color choice for another of Roger's clients, Italian couturier Valentino. Since green is one of Valentino's favourite colors, he was quite specific about wanting to use it in the London house that

Roger Banks-Pye decorated for him with Tom Parr. Valentino did not want chintz, but he had approached Colefax and Fowler because he wanted English style and top quality and, interestingly, the English understanding of comfort. In contrast to the cooler tones of the Greens' bedroom, the treatment here is far more opulent: green-and-white checked silk

Somewhat in the French manner, the same printed fabric is used for the walls, draperies, sofa, and the cushions. The headboard and the valance have separate slipcovers—the sort of extra detail that makes a pretty and practical addition. The gilt-lined black heavy paper shade on the wall lamp over the sofa picks up on the black-and-gold framed botanical prints on the opposite wall, which in themselves echo the flowery theme.

lines the walls of the drawing room, painted green bookcases are gilded, a huge sofa is covered in dark green dress velvet. Roger believes it is "an Italian idea of what English comfort is all about, and probably ten times more opulent than most Englishmen would consider. But it works. It's a visual kaleidoscope and it's magical."

Red

Red, the color of Chinese temples, and of traditional American barns, is a strong color that needs careful distribution in a room. Introducing red as an accent color to heighten the effect of the other colors in a room works only if the red is suitably softened to a paler tone to prevent it from screaming out its presence. Dark tones, ranging from rust through deep crimson, cannot be handled gingerly. However they are used, they will instantly draw the eye, and so they need to be treated boldly and used over a large expanse such as the walls or draperies. Red works well in rooms that are used mainly at night and so are viewed by lamplight and candlelight, such as dining rooms and bedrooms; the warm tones reflect the light and cast out an intense glow like firelight.

A strongly defined red color scheme needs positive and assured handling. Success rests on obtaining the right shade of color and depth of the translucent paint glaze. As a background for a collection of 18th-century pottery figures and jugs (right), the color Roger refers to as "raspberry sorbet" is perfect.

Neutral

One of Roger's primary concerns when deciding on the decoration of any room is to create an atmosphere that is unique to that room. What sort of atmosphere that might be is inflenced by many things—the dimensions of the room, the amount of natural light, the use it is put to—but one of the greatest decorative factors dictating a mood is the color scheme. When you want to create a space with a tranquil, calming feel, the ideal choice is a neutral palette. The look does not have to be one-dimensional or monotonous; the spectrum of neutrals ranges from cream with brown tones through whites such as ivory, oyster, and pearl to metallic blues and grays. The palest paint colors for walls are created by using powdered pigments in a paint base for a chalky effect. Browns are softened into butterscotch and caramel, blues are silvered to a steely edge, and dark terracotta is paled to the color of dry plaster skim. On different surfaces—wood, paper, cotton, linen, plaster—colors will take on different depths of tone, and this contrast is seen at its most effective when color schemes are kept muted. Bright colors are distracting and can prevent the eye from taking in subtle changes in

texture. The best fabrics to choose from are those that really come into their own when left in their natural state, unbleached, fresh from the mill. Linen, cotton, wool, and flannel all demonstrate a wealth of fantastic weaves, and have the added bonus of being wonderfully tactile. On the floor lay undyed tufted wool rugs for a luxurious feel.

What makes Roger's monochrome rooms so effective is the lack of that vivid color shot—what other decorators call color accents— that can, when used unwisely, make the whole scheme seem contrived. He avoids fragmenting space by breaking it up into too many different colors, and keeps to shades of ecru, ivory and cream for draperies and walls, with subtle, muted shades of other colors such as blues for slip-

covers and floor coverings. (One of his favorite shades, which he finds a versatile stand-by in many color schemes, is a subtle shade of pale brown that John Fowler referred to as "mouseback".) To complete the monochrome feel, he will distribute the same shades of white and cream used on the walls in ornaments and objects around the room,

*A **monochrome palette** is an ideal choice for a study area because it creates a restful and calm atmosphere, providing few distractions. A desk has been positioned near the window in this inviting hallway (opposite) in order to receive the maximum amount of light.*

There are no harsh colors to jar the eye in this delightful room (below). The mood is one of complete relaxation.

including his favorite creamware plates and urns, white plaster of Paris vases, whitewashed rustic baskets, and parchment lampshades. But, in common with other decorators, he will never use pure white paint in a room, since its effect is only to make other shades of white appear muddy. This is something to watch out for particularly in a room where there is art hung on the walls: the backgrounds and mats of most paintings will have faded over time and the stark contrast of pure white is not flattering. To avoid making your paintings look muddy, bring all of the colors down a shade or two to match.

There is nothing more disruptive to the coloring in a room than a pure white ceiling: it will throw out the entire balance of a room, so Roger will always use a cream-toned paint to simulate an antique white. He will use the same shade to disguise and knock back architectural detailing, for the same soothing effect. A long plate rack running above an inglenook fireplace, for example, would have been unduly prominent left in its natural wooden state. Painted the same cream as the walls, its subtle shadowing can be appreciated. You will never see a plain white door in a room Roger has decorated. He is a great believer in the 18th-century French style of using three different shades of white on the paneling and framework, a tradition that was also religiously observed by John Fowler. Taking this principle even further, Roger will sometimes use a fourth white on a particularly complex door. He will paint shadow lines on the architrave and the frame and narrow pencil lines in the molding to highlight the three-dimensional relief. "All I am doing is emphasizing nature. It is time consuming but it's worth it. Once you've seen it, you'll never go back to an ordinary flat white door," he says.

Highlighting architectural detailing by using three or four tones of white, off-white, and slate gray is particularly effective when the door and architrave are surrounded by a graphic pattern on the walls. Applied paper and paint effects have been used to create a light-hearted interpretation of stone blocks (below and opposite) and alternate narrow and wide stripes (below right).

Roger has had fun with this door (right). Further embellishing the detailing, he has painted a faux bird's-eye maple effect in pale blue in the panels and on the door jamb. Laid on top of the paint, it is obviously not meant to be a convincing wood effect. Rather, it is another example of Roger playing with decorative devices and using them in unconventional ways.

The Bold
Background

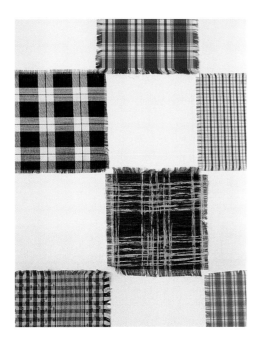

$\mathcal{W}\,a\,l\,l\,s$

$\mathcal{W}$alls, by their sheer expanse, offer some of the most exciting design possiblities in a room. Many decorators use the walls as a mere backdrop; they coat them in neutral coats of paint so that they almost disappear and concentrate their efforts on other elements in a room. But for Roger Banks-Pye, the wall treatment in a room—the choice of color and the texture—sets the entire mood of an interior. Imagine a Vuillard without those full-blown florals the color of tea roses, or a Hockney portrait of the 1970s without the psychedelic patterned background. Paints, papers, and fabrics are all conventional wall coverings, but the ways in which Roger uses them are anything but commonplace: painted surfaces are intensely colored, layer upon layer, before glazing, or else they are rubbed to a soft patina with gesso; torn sheets of blue-and-white handmade Japanese rice paper are pasted in an acreage of checkerboard along a long entrance hall; fabrics are simply tented and gathered in soft felted folds.

Ideas that are inspirational, can, at the same time, be surprisingly simple. When faced with the decoration of a rural hunting lodge, Roger avoided the most obvious response to the Scottish Highland setting of the house, which would have been broad sweeps of tartan. Yet his

Three unusual and graphic effects, none of them conventional wall finishes. Squares of blue rice paper (left) and checked linen tacked directly onto the walls (right) both make impressive effects in two very different entrance halls. Checked fabric samples are spray-mounted onto Roger's bathroom wall (above) for an amusing and easily copied idea.

graphic treatment of the long entrance hall still has strongly Scottish connotations. Roger made a feature of the walls, exaggerating their length and the uninterrupted view along the full front of the house. From baseboard to ceiling he pasted giant squares of blue Japanese rice paper onto a white painted background, starting in the middle and working outward in both directions. Suggesting the decorative hand-blocked grid patterns of the turn-of-the-century Glasgow architect Charles Rennie Mackintosh, this striking treatment is entirely appropriate to the location of the lodge.

The designer's signature blue-and-white color scheme was central to another equally original wall treatment. An entire run of an edition of silk screen prints of George Washington had been pasted directly onto the walls of a bedroom and surrounded by a lurid shade of pink paint. They could not be removed without damaging them, and the American owner was keen to preserve them. So Roger devised a contemporary equivalent of an old-fashioned print room. To cover up the offending pink and to unify the scheme, he decided to cover the room in fabric, a geometric checked weave which picked out the colors in the prints.

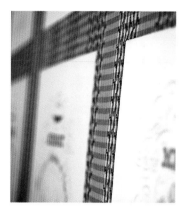

Sheets of Japanese rice paper pasted onto hall walls (above) make a dynamic entrance. Roger tore the sides of the sheets against a steel ruler to give softened edges (top right). The squares were pasted straight onto the walls.

Rectangles are cut from a gentle geometric weave to frame silk screen prints of George Washington (left and top left).

"Always scale up, not down. Everyone is terrified of making things too big—if in doubt make it bigger, not smaller."

Spray mounting squares of fabric *to the walls of the bathroom of his flat (above right) took very little time, but Roger first frayed the edges of each piece with drawn-thread work, which was a laborious task. The blue-and-white checked theme, emphasized by the checkerboard layout, is carried over to the towels and to the china, which was picked up cheaply at local junk shops.*

After measuring out the walls and the position of the prints, he then cut a rectangular "window" for each of the prints in the fabric before pasting it directly onto the walls, so that the whole room is cocooned. For a neat finish and to give a subtle three-dimensional effect, he folded in the raw edges around each print.

Fabric also provided the inspiration for an idiosyncratic wall treatment in the designer's own bathroom. Taking a light hearted approach, Roger found an ingenious way to use some of the various samples of fabric designs he had acquired along the way in his decorating career. Each of the designs he selected showed a checked pattern in some form, whether bold plain squares, a finely woven plaid, or a strongly graphic grid pattern, all in his favorite blue and white. Taking inspiration from this checkerboard theme, he pasted squares of the fabrics corner to corner onto a white background. The result is a charming patchwork effect which works on two levels. The different samples act as a very original gallery of textiles, each piece interesting in itself. And the overall effect is fresh and attractive, with a strongly textured feel that is very appealing.

Playing with texture in this way is one of Roger's favorite approaches to wall treatments, and he is very ready to experiment and work with the most unpromising of materials in order to achieve different effects. That formidable reminder of the 1970s, orange burlap wallpaper, had been pasted onto the walls of a large sunny dining room. The initial reaction of most decorators would be to strip the walls completely and start with a clean slate. Not Roger Banks-Pye: he rose to the difficult challenge of working with what he had, to come up with a successful wall treatment. He left the burlap in place and painted the walls white, then sandpapered lightly over the whole wall in order to loosen the surface and bring out fibrous flecks in the fabric. Finally, several coats of buttery-yellow paint were applied to make a vivid background. The result is a uniquely textured finish that could not have been created by using any of the traditional methods.

Different occupants require very different types of wall surfaces. In a house where there are children, the wall covering must be able to withstand the knocks and marks that are inevitably caused by the constant wear and tear of young people. In such situations there is no need to make aesthetic compromises—it is possible to devise attractive and original finishes that are also resilient. Roger created just such a finish for a large dining room adjoining an open-plan kitchen in a family house where there are three small children. The walls were first painted a shade of deep red to form the background. Parchment paper, cut out in rectangular-shaped stone-sized blocks with roughly torn edges, was

> *"Painted walls always look better with some layered depth, either through applied paint or a plaster technique to add texture."*

A practical family dining room *walled with torn slabs of parchment over deep-red painted grouting (right). Details are never sacrificed to the larger elements: the baseboard (below) is painted to extend the floor, and the cornice (above) is highlighted in shades of stone and bone.*

then pasted over the top. The effect is that of giant-scale brickwork with irregular red grouting, such as might appear in a child's drawing of a house. Several layers of varnish seal the surface for protection. A similar design could have been painted directly onto the walls using a *trompe l'oeil* effect, but it would have been less convincing because the texture of the fake brickwork would have been absent. It is in this sort of painstaking attention to detail to ensure he creates the exact effect he is after that Roger excels.

As in any room that Roger decorates, other details in the room echo the walls. Cream linen draperies are overstitched with bands of heavy crimson-and-white checked cotton cut into wide stripes to complement the masonry effect. To echo the ragged edges of the paper "bricks" on the walls, the edges of the checked band bordering the valance are frayed to the depth of three rows in the check design. The full effect is appreciated at its best when seen against the light shining through the window.

In a Roger Banks-Pye interior, painted surfaces are seldom solidly washed with flat latex or decorated in just one color. Colors are applied over other tonal shades, then buffed to a burnished glow. By combining colorwashing and sponging, it is also possible to achieve a loose imitation of some of the textures and colors found on old colorwashed plaster walls. White egg-shell paint is usually the opaque base for transparent washes, thinned with mineral spirits. Subtlety is essential for the finished effect to be successful; there should never be too strong a contrast between the colors or they will fight

Using illusion to create atmosphere, Roger has draped the walls of his drawing room with tea-stained drip-dried fabric as a backdrop to his eclectic furnishings and decorative objects (left). Treating fabric with tea to create an antique finish was a technique often used by Nancy Lancaster, and now enthusiastically revived by Roger.

Crewelwork fabric with an unusual blue background is also simply nailed to his bedroom walls in what Roger calls a "cavalier fashion." Clients, of course, would expect and receive a more professional battened finish.

each other. Richness of tone is achieved by leaving gaps in the sponged and washed coats so that each layer shows through. The finish to strive for is one in which the layers merge naturally, and the meeting between them becomes indistinguishable.

Roger's belief that you can change the whole atmosphere and mood of a room merely by tackling the wall treatment is best seen in his own apartment. Researching those travelers who turn their souvenir hunting into exotic decoration at home, *House & Garden* magazine approached Roger Banks-Pye to photograph him at home with the ram's-head marquetry chairs that he had had shipped from Jaipur. This inspired him to introduce more Indian influences into his apartment. For an instant effect he chose a cotton fabric with Mogul miniatures printed on a white background and pinned it to the walls at one end of his drawing room. But first he soaked the fabric in a bathtub of Assam tea to soften the glaze and stain it lightly to subdue the brightness of the background color. Once it had lost that newness and looked slightly antiquated, instead of ironing out the creases, he hung up the wet

fabric to achieve a draped effect. Without a lining, unhemmed, just folded over at the edges and tacked with upholstery nails to the wall, the hanging brought instant effect. It has a spontaneous and temporary charm. But Roger is aware that he could get away with such casual methods only in his own

home. "Clients are wary if you suggest tackling a project in such a cavalier way. They want a top-quality finish and that would have defeated the point."

Such a bold pattern as the Mogul design could easily serve as the focal point in a room, but it is treated just like any other

conventional wall covering and hung with pictures, so that it acts as a good backdrop to unrelated objects in the room. This is an excellent demonstration of the way pattern can be used to unify a scheme. An even bolder move is to run pattern wall-to-wall and floor to ceiling, unbroken even at the

Overall pattern is an effective disguise *for awkwardly shaped rooms or where space is limited such as in the top-floor bedroom (above). The trailing design of honeysuckle helps to hide the odd angles on the ceiling caused by the sloping eaves, to create a cozy rather than a claustrophobic*

ambiance. To be truly effective the pattern should be used as comprehensively as it is here: on the walls, at the window, on the headboard, bedspread and valance, and even the back of the door (left), to achieve a seamless transition between different surfaces.

The diminutive size of these two bathrooms *(above) is overridden by the bold all-over pattern. The window treatments are kept deliberately simple so as not to draw attention to their strange proportions; flat pull-down and Roman shades act almost as an extension of the walls.*

windows, where the same fabric that lines the walls is used for the draperies and shades too. A pattern that, when viewed on a small scale such as in a pattern book, can appear almost overbearing can—provided that the colors are not shrill and the design decisive—almost disappear when used in such a comprehensive manner.

An applied pattern can also serve to solve awkward problems—where the proportions of a room are less than perfect, for example. In one windowless attic bedroom, where the only natural light came from the skylight in the roof directly over the bed and one tiny window on the dressing-room landing, Roger had to devise a scheme to lighten and

brighten the room. In order to focus on the skylight, and to detract from the lack of windows, he had the walls painted a soft yellow. A design of branches and foliage painted white, inspired by crewelwork, twines simply along the wraparound windowless walls, ever upward to the overhead skylight that makes the yellow glow.

Roger rarely uses wallpapers, preferring to employ more unusual treatments. But this most ubiquitous of wall coverings, when used in a design that incorporates vertical stripes, can serve a particular purpose: to make a small room appear larger. Broad bands of bold color with a pinstripe between take the eye upward and direct it toward the

broad expanse of the ceiling to give the illusion of spaciousness all around, rather than allowing the eye to focus immediately upon the furniture and other objects in the room. This method of visually opening up a room is far preferable to the conventional practice of painting a dark room plain white. If a room receives little natural sunlight anyway, there is no benefit in struggling to maximize that poor-quality light. The results are more often

than not cold, clinical, and unwelcoming. Far better to use strong, dark colors to create a warm atmosphere.

The effect of both of these principles—using vertical stripes and deep colors—is demonstrated in the dark dining room of a narrow town house in which the walls are covered in a deep red self-woven stripe of heavy silk damask. The dark maroon chevron stripe covers the walls above the dado, the

"Always make a dark room darker. You can paint a dark room white, but it will still be dark, and if it is a room mostly used at night, such as a dining room, rather give it atmosphere with deep intense colour that works well in artificial light."

A richly colored interior *creates a warm, club-style atmosphere for entertaining (far left). Leather upholstery on the seats of the dining chairs, deeply patinated with age, and a highly polished shine on the mahogany table reflect the low light from the window by day and the glow from the firelight and candles by night. Two wing chairs add a cozy note.*

The dado is painted off-white *to lift the intense wall color of the heavy silk (above). The woven herringbone design in the stripe enhances the vertical, while the silk braid with a subtle looped fringe neatens the junction between the walls and the chair rail. The baseboard (left) is stippled grey to anchor the walls to the floor.*

Not all wall treatments are serious. *Sometimes Roger enjoys a little irreverence. In the bedroom in the basement of Valentino's London house (left), the walls are covered in a charcoal-colored* toile de Jouy *on a cream background featuring monkeys clambering on trees. In the adjoining bathroom (above) the* toile *design is picked out in gilt on the black panel at the side of the bathtub. For a personal touch that would slip by unnoticed by all but the keenest eye, the image depicts a monkey sitting on a branch that is holding out two intertwined Gs, the initials of Giancarlo Giammetti, Chairman of the Board of Valentino S.p.A. Maintaining the simian theme, black-framed prints of monkeys hang on the walls of the bedroom. A black-and-red color scheme unifies the two rooms and the black-and-gilt bedroom furniture and bathroom fixtures were specially designed to complement the grand 19th-century Russian bed, the focal point of the room. A handsome sofa with deep, plump cushions covered in a large-scale paisley design and a deeply fringed and tasseled edging reinforces the luxurious and handsome milieu.*

edges neatly finished across the top of the chair rail and below the cornice by bands of silk ribbon in the same color. This rich covering provides a perfect foil to the black-and-white gilt-framed engravings. The fabric for the draperies, a rich paisley design, picks out the color of the walls, while underfoot the specially woven maroon-and-blue patterned carpet unifies the whole scheme.

A similarly deep red in another house was achieved by a different method. There, the walls were washed with shades of vermilion, terracotta, and crimson paint, then glazed. The porcelain-like translucency of the finish forms a perfect contemporary backdrop for a collection of 18th-century pottery figures.

All of Roger Banks-Pye's wall treatments make statements and the walls serve as the main factor in a room for setting the scene. But his use of fabric as loose wall hangings enables him perhaps to make his most dramatic gestures. Hanging fabric from walls loosely in this way has the instant effect of providing two ingredients in a room which are vital to Roger: atmosphere and comfort.

Informally tented layers of lighter fabrics give a nomadic feel, a look Roger used to good effect in his living room when he selected the Mogul print to give the illusion of a temporarily pitched tent. Rich hangings of weightier fabrics, such as plush velvets and heavy watered silks, when ornately draped, can conjure up an altogether different atmosphere. Reminiscent of the elaborate stage curtains of Victorian theaters and music halls, they never fail to evoke a dramatic mood.

Wall hangings provide an opportunity to use fabric on a large scale, in wider expanses

"Though there are moments when plain white walls might seem a relief, those moments are rare, and should be discouraged."

This style of felt tenting *was inspired by Thomas Hope, the 19th-century neoclassical furniture designer, and this luxurious and warm mustard cocoon was created by John Stephanidis. Roger has added a black-and-white checked bedcover and the walls, carpet, woodwork and valance are all velvety brown moleskin which anchors the yellow and ensures a strong, masculine result.*

than on even the biggest of windows. Without needing to be drawn back during the day, they can act as permanent flat canvases. Any pattern can be viewed and appreciated as it is meant to be seen, uninterrupted by tassels and tiebacks, and so it is an ideal way of

displaying large-scale designs which can easily get lost on tightly pleated draperies. Conversely, an entire room draped in a single fabric in one solid color can look amazing, particularly when the color is a strong one, such as the mustard yellow Roger chose for the hanging of the walls in one bedroom, which looks wonderful in artificial light.

Loose wall hangings are far more tactile than any other type of wall covering. The range of different textures available is huge, far greater than fabric that is pasted to the walls, where the choice is limited to lighter weights. The comfort factor of being surrounded by soft, flexible materials, which move gently as you brush past, is enormous.

In a larger room, tenting just part of it is a useful technique when you want to define a section for a particular purpose. A dining table and chairs may be set at one end of a living room; fabric draped around them will help to define the boundaries of the dining area. Even tenting just a small section can be effective. A comfortable armchair, set into a corner with a table placed conveniently at hand for a drink and a book, can be cocooned around two walls to create a private retreat.

Bedrooms lend themselves particularly to this treatment. Historically, four-poster beds were surrounded with thick layers of fabric to provide warmth. In older houses where the heating may be less than efficient, wall hangings can provide practical comfort. Felt, with its insulating qualities, or chintz, lined to give it volume before hanging, is an ideal choice when the cold is a factor. But even in heated houses hanging fabric is an easy way to add a touch of luxury.

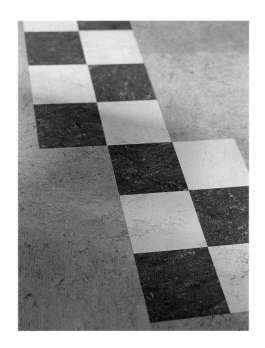

Floors

*T*here is a decorating maxim that flooring which makes the least fuss makes the strongest impression. This is quite erroneous, in Roger's opinion. Perhaps because floors are the largest surface area in a house, and so present a rather daunting challenge, people tend to play safe and opt for very conventional treatments, concentrating their imaginative efforts on the walls and windows. So floors are muffled in acres of anonymous tufted wool in solid colors, or oceans of sisal and coir, and entirely ignored. But in the skilful hands of an imaginative designer, floors can emerge from decorating obscurity.

"Seagrass was the eighties answer to sixties haircord," says Roger. "It's like reading the same old stories over again. I first saw coconut matting in 1970, and it still goes down all over the world, even though you scratch your knees and ruin your pantyhose. You should never be afraid when planning the floor covering. When I see seagrass or beige haircord I know that it's a perfectly good, cheap, and safe flooring alternative, but I know also that the clients are scared."

***Staircases provide an opportunity** for characterful carpet design because they are contained within a very particular framework. A trompe l'oeil star design (left), intricately shadowed for a three-dimensional effect, is set in a deep blue sky whose color is picked up in the stair posts.*

***When your stair carpet has a distinct motif,** why not continue it in painted form on the surrounding stair treads (right).*

***Abstract designs cut from linoleum floor covering** can make interesting patterns. If your geometry is not up to it, use pre-cut tiles (above).*

Highly patterned floor coverings give a rhythmic flow to every style of interior. In Roger's apartment, he knew chintz would be unsuitable at his bedroom windows, so he stuck it directly onto the floorboards instead (left). Handsome blonde wood furniture, crisp blue-and-white fabrics, and crewelwork upholstered onto the walls are pulled together by the strong pattern on the floor. Tough and resilient, despite its lack of sealer, the fabric copes easily with wear.

Different interiors determine his choice. In his own flat in London he has had the freedom to try out choices for floor coverings that are far from obvious options, including materials that are more commonly considered for curtains and walls. As an experiment, he pasted a classic Colefax and Fowler chintz with a black background onto a large board. He laid the board on the floor in the Colefax showroom at 39 Brook Street, like a doormat, and then invited people to walk over it. The fabric survived this cavalier treatment, so he duly glued it down on the bare floorboards in his bedroom, without sealer. Practically speaking, it is a surprisingly feasible option: the coloring and design are ideal choices as they do not show any marks. The whole surface is easily swept clean, and the fabric is thick enough to withstand the relatively light foot traffic that a bedroom receives. And the texture is unique—as flat as painted floorboards but with a visible weave: the overall effect is nothing like that achieved with any other type of floor covering. Yard for yard it cost more than a carpet, but five years later it still looks fine. Roger now has plans to devise a scheme for a bedroom using a wide chintz border on a white rug, and plain white draperies lined with the same chintz.

> *"I've discovered that patterned carpet when it's laid on the floor, depending on its color, will have the same effect as a plain one."*

Of course, you cannnot lay chintz in every house. Conventional flooring treatments are popular for the very reason that in most cases they do their job supremely well. But flooring solutions do not always have to be grand carpets. Even when using common-place materials Roger will give them a new twist. Ordinary rush matting tiles stitched together and laid wall to wall would have looked too countrified in a companionable dining room with buttery walls and light-filled windows. The blue-and-white checked fabric and china that are a key factor in the decoration were the inspiration for the flooring: Roger inked in every other square with blue marker pens to form a checkerboard pattern. When the surface color starts to fade from the contant scuffing of shoes and boots it will be an easy matter to repaint it. This simple technique, which requires no specialist skills, transforms basic rush matting. "Pay attention to details and people will appreciate the atmosphere in a room," advises Roger.

Contrasts create surprises. To link the two sides of a double drawing room, with butterscotch painted walls that glow in layers of sunlit yellow at one end and deep blue walls

Floor treatments deserve as much attention to detail as any other area of decoration, and this is especially true at the physical junction with other elements in the room. Mitered corners are painstakingly constructed from a specially woven carpet border, so that the pattern continues uninterrupted around an awkward window (right), while the graphic design seen above is complemented by the bold blue stripe of the binding on a floor-length tablecloth.

A little imagination and artistic flair can improve on humble materials. Sisal and rush matting can be customized with a double width of contrasting binding tape or inked-in squares (opposite), while floorboards can be transformed by the application of a painted design into a unique border for antique rugs (above left).

at the other, the floorboards are stained black. Natural sisal matting in a neutral shade is laid on top. But once again, rather than leaving plain matting unadorned, Roger has made a subtle adjustment which makes a huge difference and lifts the flooring treatment out of the ordinary. The sisal is bound throughout in a double border, in narrow black, then in a wider band of blue, which looks stylish and smart against the black boards. The clever distribution of blue and yellow in the two rooms is anchored because of that strong flooring, which pulls together two very individual schemes.

Flooring treatments have to address different areas and needs with the material and the pattern used, even within the same house. Using comparatively inexpensive sisal matting rugs in the drawing room allowed for a major investment in a heavy-duty carpet for the stairs, which get heavy traffic in a household with small children. A bold pattern of ivory-shaded stars on a bright blue background, edged with a band of white in reverse contrast to the dark edging of the matting, carries this graphic statement through to the rest of the house.

Twenty-five years ago, when Roger was starting the decoration of his country house, he could not afford to use the famous Colefax and Fowler patterned carpets that he longed for. So he improvised. "It amused me one evening in the study to stay up until 4 a.m. painting the floorboards black and then stenciling them with red-and-cream Colefax medallions around the edge. There was no painstaking preparation—it was all done on the spur of a moment to gratify a whim. Now that it looks a bit chipped and worn it's

wonderful." He had to paint in the shadows by hand. This kind of fastidious attention to detail makes things look less contrived, rather as though they have fallen together happily. Now the painted border makes a distinctive frame for rugs laid on top.

In another house early in his career he painted the floorboards with white gloss paint—one coat only, which quickly wore back to the wood until there was just a scraping of white like a bleached-out boat deck. He then put in camel-hair sofas and chairs slipcovered in gray flannel. Once they were in position, he made up his own rug with thick

The appeal of checks in their many forms for Roger is their strong graphic quality. Taken to their extreme, dark blue squares on an off-white background form a stark grid on the floor.

The shape and design of these rag runners define the movement of traffic in this attic corridor, while the painted grid on the far wall beyond the doorway punctuates the space at the end of the view.

natural burlap squares frayed and sewn together. "Checkerboards gave a precise pattern in contrast with the irregular white boards, and we simply nailed down the burlap patchwork with bronze upholstery nails. It cost virtually nothing."

Later he discovered the luxury of laying Colefax patterned carpets wall-to-wall with matching borders specially woven to fit the contours of irregularly shaped rooms. He now uses pattern with supreme confidence, and is adept at persuading clients who are wary of overwhelming a room with a strong design underfoot to be brave in their choice of floor covering. He knows that the effect of even the most vibrant of designs is subordinated when it is used on a large scale, so that it is not overpowering. But the overall rhythmic movement that a pattern provides helps to give a room a dynamic edge. This fact becomes obvious in David Green's bedroom, which has pattern upon pattern, with green-and-white roses on the walls and at the windows. The floor has a strong overall pattern of leaves and twining tendrils.

Because the colors are so closely toned in shades of gray and green, and the weight of pattern is evenly distributed between floors and walls, the strong carpet does not create tension in the room. What it does add, that a solid-colored carpet would not, is a sense of movement, helping the eye to travel around and up, rather than coming to an abrupt stop when it comes to the floor. The same design is used with equal effect in the bedroom of another house, this time in a yellow colorway to tone with golden walls painted with a white flowering tree.

It was his country home that instilled in Roger a passion for patterned floors and started him on his mission. Apart from his exercises in floor painting for decoration, he would layer many different rugs and runners on top of one another on the old wooden floors. Practicality, which often informs Roger's decisions, was also a consideration. "I suspect that there were only so many layers because there was nowhere else to conveniently store the rugs," he admits. "Twenty carpets layered on boards look marvelous. It doesn't matter a damn if people come indoors in muddy boots; they don't seem to get dirty. I don't want the house to look like a Mayfair drawing room and I don't want to worry about mud and burn marks from spitting fires."

Layering rugs upon rugs in a spacious room is effective because many patterns placed together resolve their differences. Roger will often cannibalize old rugs and sections of old carpet to make up new shapes and designs for variety. For the drawing room in his country house he made one big rug using a Colefax medallion on a cream background. He will mix different textures, such as strips of old woolen rugs with cotton rag runners from the Dominican Republic sewn together. In shades of ice and denim, they have faded to form a large repeat pattern underfoot. In one house he and the client created an off-white rag rug from pieces rescued from a damaged 17th-century Agra carpet.

"Old rugs are right in any house," says Roger. For a photographic shoot for *The World of Interiors* magazine he once borrowed a rug which was just perfect for his London apartment. Unfortunately the price tag was $75,000 so the rug was duly returned after the shoot. Instead, he found a old long runner and laid it down in the middle of the room, where it still is today. It works as a stylish and unusual link between the seating group around the fireplace and the table and chairs at the other end of the room. It is successful only because it is centred. Roger is as precise about its placement as he is about its function.

Windows

More than any other decorative element, the handling of window treatments has become the most dramatic and important showpiece of the decorator's skills. John Fowler was the greatest British exponent of the art of window treatments in recent history, and the draperies and bed hangings he designed remain supreme examples of the understanding of cut, construction, and proportion. He also had a passion for seeking out sources for fabric with which to generally increase the decorative range, and his diligence resulted in the discovery of many decorative historical documents that have become the cornerstone of Colefax and Fowler's range.

In these last few decades, it seems decorators have continually researched and exploited every style available, to produce ever more complex confections of fabric, shape, and detailing in their curtains and draperies. This has resulted in varying degrees of success. The worst offenders have often disregarded the architectural grammar of the room and produced draperies of inexpert cut and haphazard finish. The best have an intrinsic understanding of the propriety of their

These beautifully proportioned draperies at a drawing room window may look simple at first glance but are actually immensely complex in technical detail (left and right). The choice of chintz for the inner draw draperies rather than the stationary panels, a reversal of the usual practice, is unusual and effective. Here they are handsomely lined in a red check (above). Deep concave rods supporting outlined taffeta dress curtains show only a splash of the chintz draperies behind. The marvellous scale of the composition creates a grand effect without resorting to the more usual swags and cascades.

design, so that full consideration is given to how it will work with the room's scale and the client's taste. Thought is given to the appropriate selection of fabric pattern, color and, trimmings. When a pair of draperies of complex design made in the finest fabrics may cost as much as $50,000, drapery design becomes a very serious subject.

Today, given the restraints on most people's purses, together with the general trend toward simplification in decoration, many interior designers are paring down and using less fabric and fewer trimmings. But, as with all trends, there are those who buck them. Roger Banks-Pye is one who manages to maintain a workable balance in his designs between whimsy and practicality, between financial consideration and perfect detailing, and between benefiting from the expertise of the craftsmen he works with while breathing new life into traditional methods and designs.

He had plenty of opportunity to experiment with drapery designs when he dressed the Colefax and Fowler shop windows. Here he learned about cut, style, and proportion

and tried out all sorts of designs. He learned so well that when it came to the real thing, he had the confidence and expertise to deal with very complicated designs. The beautiful draperies he designed for the drawing room shown on the previous pages are evidence of his mature accomplishment and a good example of his sure handling of color, design, and finish. The double draperies hang from a deeply concave rod, which gives shape at ceiling height where there is no deadlight above the window frame and therefore no

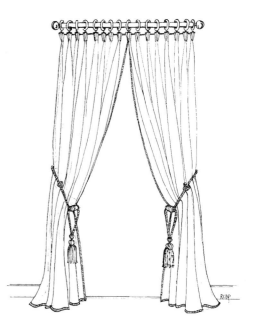

room for a valance. The unlined taffeta panels are held in place with Italian stringing and give the effect of an extended valance overlying the draw curtains behind. Roger shows great assurance in the choice of fabrics, with a bold check-lined chintz which contrasts strongly with the muted colors of the striped taffeta. The stationary panels are bound along the top, and both sets of draperies are finished with two different kinds of neat fringing on their leading edges.

A sophisticated design concept such as this would be almost impossible to convey to a client verbally, but Roger's artistic talent allows him to communicate his ideas easily through his sketches. Because of their technical precision and full details, including the exact form of curtain rod; these also convey information clearly to the makers. Indeed, he is so fascinated by the intricate and all-important construction process that he takes great pleasure in regularly visiting the workrooms to see his draperies, slipcovers, and upholstery being cut or assembled, which is something more decorators should do.

Communicating window treatment designs to his clients is easy for Roger because he draws so well. The sketches shown here are for very simple window treatments, such as for the situation shown opposite, where he uses unlined cream linen with a small French-pleated heading. Simple tassels are appropriate as tiebacks.

Very simple painted rings and poles are most suitable for hanging this style of drapery, though there is room for elaboration, such as using tapes of contrasting fabric as ties to secure the drapery to the pole. More ornate poles can be formed from wrought iron, which gives the flexibility of curves and fancy finials (left).

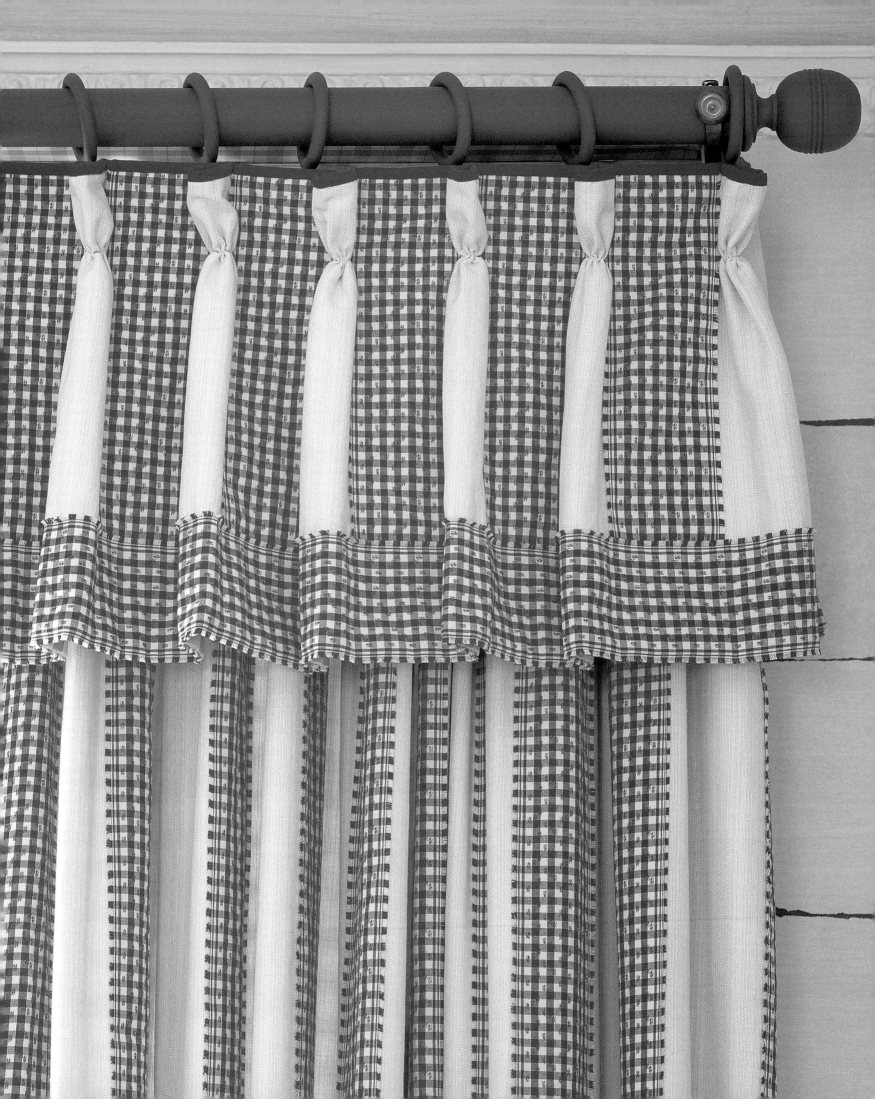

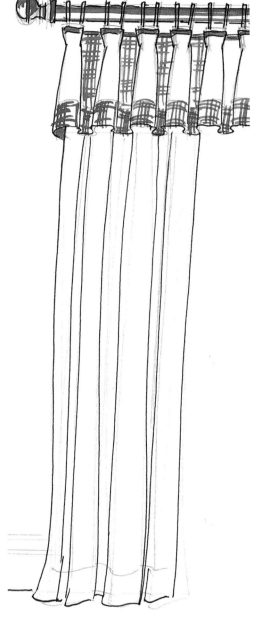

Roger loves to add elements of surprise and wit to his designs, as is evident in the fun he has with overlaid frayed fabrics. A fascination for fraying the edges of fabric and then applying them in squares or strips to other fabrics started years ago when he experimented with the frayed squares of checked fabric which he glued to his bathroom wall. He developed this idea further in his experiments with appliquéd fabric on curtains and draperies in his London and country homes. The drapes in the breakfast room in his country house were a precursor to other designs. Roger bought about 100 checked napkins, frayed

their edges, and then had them sewn onto plain white linen to produce the checkerboard effect. Another design was for some draperies of plain heavy linen weave with applied strips of red check with frayed edges. Because of these curtains and the room's "stone block" wall effect, Roger calls it his Flintstone Look. The result is certainly witty and informal, but the use of high-quality fabrics and the perfect execution means that the effect is not at all shabby. Again experimenting with a different method of applying fabric onto fabric, he designed draperies with stemmed roses cut out from chintz and

Always look for new ways to use fabric and tell a story. Roger's ideas evolve during the sketching process, which is a vital time to see whether his designs will work, both visually and technically. Playing with the idea of using stripes of checked fabric laid onto a plain background, he came up with the design shown left, with its elaborate curved rod. The same basic idea was the principle behind the very much simpler arrangement sketched above.

The finished article shows how effective the use of overlaid fabric, incorporating a frayed edging, can be (opposite). Such a design could quite easily be adapted in a simpler form.

blanket stitched onto natural linen draperies, whose edges were finished with an appliquéd border of checked fabric. The simple French-pleated headings had a plain binding and little bunches of appliquéd roses.

Roger would not wish to lay claim to being the inventor of the styles of window treatment described here, but simply says that he tries to bring a fresh twist to whatever scheme he is working on. One of his signature notes is to line draperies with contrasting fabric, his view being that with the backs of draperies visible to the outside world, every pair of draperies on that façade should present a uniform front so that the whole house "reads" as one. He usually uses his beloved checks, very often in blue. But in one house he chose red checked linings to unify the front of the house and beige for the back.

Physical attributes are vital considerations, and this priority is applied throughout the home of Mr. and Mrs. Green. The interior architecture was influenced by the Arts and Crafts movement of the late 19th century and the tone of the house is sympathetic to the movement's belief in the stylistic unity of architecture and interior decoration. Each element in the dining room reveals superb craftsmanship and subtle elegance. There is a fine herringbone wood-block floor, simple paneling—a favored Arts and Crafts wall finish—and beautifully tailored heavy draperies hanging from rings on a wooden pole. When designing understated draperies Roger always maintains the fullness of width to provide weight and structure, which is here further emphasized by a subtle grid of over-stitching. The leaded windows rise to near

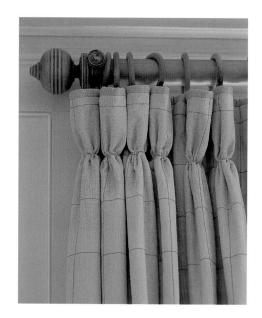

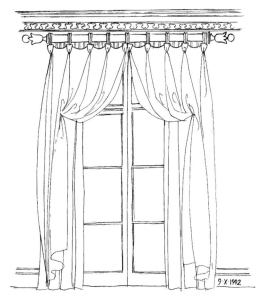

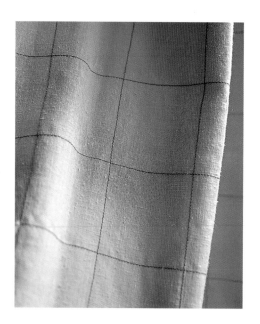

ceiling height, so in this case a valance would be doubly unsuited both because of the room's period and because too much light would be lost. There is a similar window in Roger's London residence, where he has hung unlined goblet-headed linen draperies through which the light filters pleasantly; the overall effect is smart and gentlemanly. In this case, he has used rope and tassel tiebacks to allow as much light as possible into the room, but as a rule he dislikes distorting the fall of the fabric. In his view it is essential that draperies hang like a fluid pilaster, with the valance, if there is one, mimicking the effect of an architectural capital at the top.

His grandest draperies are luxuriously opulent without being ostentatious. At his most theatrical, he reveals the attitude and application of a couturier, who would not dream of sacrificing an inch of fabric if it would be detrimental to the finished line. Where appropriate he likes to be very generous with the volume of fabric in the drops, "so they look like something you could dance with." The draperies in Valentino's drawing room, for instance, would make very suitable dancing partners. Made in the grand style, double pinked, and scalloped at the edges, they fall in a fluid sweep of taffeta.

***Minute attention to detail** and quality of workmanship ensure that even the simplest drapery designs look tailored and unique. Roger relishes the opportunity to have a change from designing draperies for formal drawing rooms and here in the dining room he has used strength of line to convey the tone of this Arts and Crafts-style house (right). A fine checked design was machine stitched over heavy linen (left). The grid is perfect, each line unwaveringly true, as satisfying to the eye as the herringbone pattern on the floor.*

A clever solution (left) copes with the problem of a wide window made up of three tall, narrow panes side by side. If the window were dressed with a single pair of draperies at either side, the center pane would be left bare when the draperies were drawn back. The solution was to treat each of the three panes as a separate window, with a curved heading fitted above each of the three panes. This allows for a more generous quantity of fabric to be used than with a flat heading, thus adding fullness. Shades behind the draperies direct the light so that it enters the room at a flatteringly low level.

French pleats echo the rounded shape of the heading (above), while the blue binding picks out the curved line. The draperies are looped back at mid-height (above left) to reveal checked shades on the upper half of the window, while the lining in a contrasting check can be seen on the lower half.

The individual treatment given to each of the three panes is repeated for the single narrow window on the far right of the wall (as seen in the sketch below), unifying a difficult arrangement of very unbalanced window shapes.

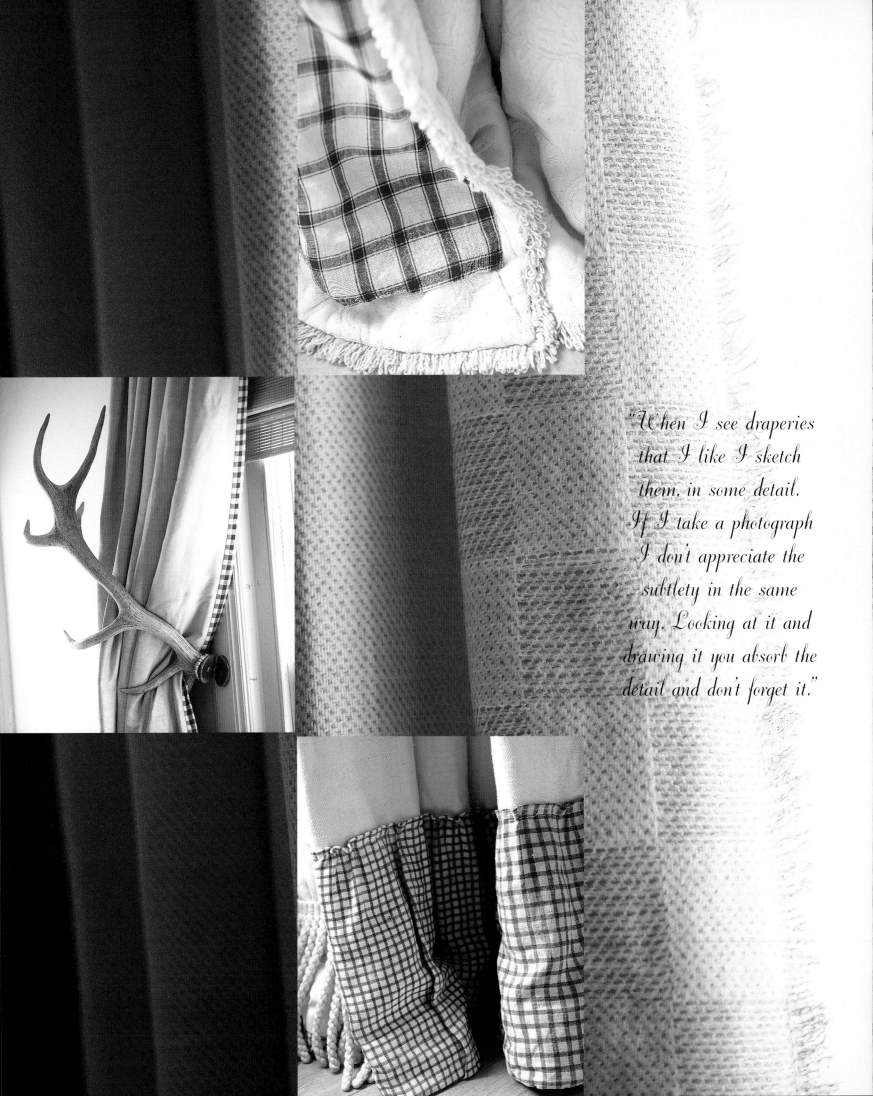

"When I see draperies that I like I sketch them, in some detail. If I take a photograph I don't appreciate the subtlety in the same way. Looking at it and drawing it you absorb the detail and don't forget it."

Generous proportions are used in a different way in Roger's proposal for the drawing room draperies in the town house shown on the previous pages. Like all the others in the street, the house has three tall, narrow windows set side by side at second-floor level. Roger observed that the neighbors had attempted to solve this problem by having a single pair of draperies on one long rod. When the draperies are drawn back, the

result is an unbecoming mass of fabric falling on either side of the windows, leaving the middle one undressed. His solution was to give each window its own pair of draperies on individual curved rods. This gives a sense of three-dimensional depth and horizontal rhythm to the floor-to-ceiling stationary panels, as well as allowing for a more ample quantity of fabric.

Roger knows well how to maximize the effect of his window treatments by finding unusual ways to mix fabrics, or perhaps using

fabrics for a different purpose than the one for which they were intended. For example, when he wants to convey a simple, chic style, he favors upholstery-weight fabrics, often in light colors, which produce a luxurious tactile quality. In one client's home, he used a pure linen for the main bedroom draperies. Integral to the design was a checked border to the valance, specially woven into the fabric and formed from contrasting squares of

Experimenting with fabric, Roger has used a woven linen (left and his original design right) for the draperies and wall covering of a bedroom. The subtle check has been frayed at the bottom of the valance and on the leading edge. Using upholstery-weight fabrics allows the self-patterned linings and fringe to play a leading role.

Adopting a similar color and fabric in different ways throughout the same house gives a sense of continuity (opposite). Blue checks are used as linings, visible when the draperies are drawn back behind antler horns and at the bottom edge. Different examples of American homespun are tacked onto the bottom edge of the back of a fringed hallway drapery to act as skirts, a welcoming treat to be viewed from outside.

caramel and neutral linen. The front edges are frayed to the depth of one complete row of squares to form its own fringe, and the same woven checked fabric is used to cover the walls. The result is soft, understated, and perfect for the situation.

Trimmings are the icing on the cake, without which the whole effect would be lost to obscurity. Roger is fastidious about his trimmings and goes to great trouble to select just the right foil in exactly the right color—"If you don't get the color right you lose the whole

thing." He always contrast binds the headings of his draperies or valances exactly ⅜ inch. He feels strongly that getting the detail right is essential to the final effect. "Binding acts like a full stop at the end of a sentence," he explains. The front edge of draperies is always finished with something, be it with fan edging, some cord, or his signature frayed edge. Valances are finished with generous fringes of suitable scale and style.

THE MAIN BEDROOM
SINGLE SMOCK HEADING TO GATHERED HEADING
FINISHED WITH CHECK BORDER AT LEADING EDGE
NATURAL LINEN BLINDS WITH HEMSTITCHED BASE
3 PAIRS OF CURTAINS.
1" FRAYED EDGE

Roger's belief is that all decorations should properly fit their given space and suit the client's lifestyle. To this end, thought is given to how his clients use their house; what sort of entertaining they do, which rooms the family will use, and so on. (There's certainly no point in having pure silk draperies where they may be vulnerable to the sticky hands of children.) An equally important consideration is that window treatments should reflect the style and spirit of the house without being inhibited by purely historical concepts.

Blue-and-white checks and stripes of various sizes and designs are combined on the floor, the bed, and for the draperies and blind at the window in this bedroom (above), for a charming patchwork effect.

A simple window treatment can be made from panels of checked cotton cut to fit (left). Neatly hemmed on all four sides and then studded with eyelets at the top corners, they can quickly be hooked in place.

Gingham napkins were frayed at the edges and then stitched onto heavy cream linen in a regular pattern (right) to create these striking and very individual draperies and valance.

Roger also applies his customary generosity of scale to the depth of valances, whose proportions relate to the scale of the room and its decorative content. Valances are usually measured at their shallowest point at three inches per twelve inches of curtain drop from rod to floor, but Roger generally allows four inches per foot. "Always, always scale up," is a Roger definition for successful design, which can be applied to drapery, pattern, or furniture. This sense of harmonic scale is well demonstrated by two sets of draperies he made for Lady Grant. The simpler of the designs is in her London drawing room,

where the valances are constructed with two deep, sculptured box pleats at either end of a serpentine valance. The front edges of the draperies have a wide contrast border so that the border matches the line of the valance pleats. Similar in concept but far more complicated in design is the dining-room treatment in her Scottish residence. Here, there is a complex serpentine rod from which falls a gathered valance with goblet pleats

and cascades, finished with a heavy bullion fringe and elegant tassels on ropes. The grace and weight of these glorious draperies complements the noble proportions of the room and its decorations. Roger has given the Grants, in his own words, "the look that creates an impression of quiet quality." Another example of this relationship is seen in the Grants' country-house bathroom. In this case, a blue chevron stripe is edged with a

The tone of this sunny drawing room *is airy and very comfortable (opposite). The cream wool draperies are trimmed with a yellow-and-bone wool bullion fringe and the box pleats (top left) give a smart, understated line which extends through to the rope-edged border (left).*

In a Scottish bathroom*, light is maximized by having high-strung draperies at the broad window (above). The use of heavy-weight fabric and dark cord braid (right) emphasizes the masculinity of this room, with its baronial feel, suggested by the tartan furnishings and trophy stag's head.*

triple-colored cord. Combined with the dark walls, tartan upholstery, and brass ceiling light, it creates a thoroughly masculine tone. In complete contrast is his choice of fabric style for Lady Grant's bedroom in Scotland, where there is a deep and curvaceous pleated valance finished with a long cotton cut fringe. The warm colors accentuate the femininity of the scheme, with the same fabric used for all the major decorative players.

Here is perfection in proportion, *style and material. Roger's grandest draperies are luxuriously opulent without ever being ostentatious. At his most theatrical, his application is that of a couturier who does not sacrifice one inch of material to the detriment of the finished line. In this case, the fluent proportions of the serpentine valance (below) are balanced by the generous column of fabric beneath and the classic dimension of the room (opposite).*

A touch of gilding is the ultimate luxury. *The golden bullion fringe and decorative tassels (far right) are complemented by the gilt band around the architrave on the adjacent door (right).*

"The first thing to do when you have hung draperies is to walk away from the window, holding up the hems. Then let the fabric fall back naturally. Never force the fabric into corrugated folds."

Two similar valances illustrate interpretations for a gathered valance skirt finished in a pretty cut fringe and held in soft pleats. The one on the left is unusual because it dips in the center rather than having two pleats on either side (above).

Designs can evolve through various stages, as the sketch below shows: this one was discarded because, having completed it, Roger decided he disliked the rather military-style epaulettes created by the curved valances on either side.

Whenever he can, Roger will take the best of classic design and turn it around to make something more inventive and individual. Inevitably, the style of drapery is somewhat related to the type of fabric selected and the technical requirements of its situation. French-pleated headings are a favorite, but he likes to have them fashioned in a lighter and looser way than usual. His other most frequently used designs are Italian-strung draperies which allow great flexibility in defining the depth of sweep and contour of draperies and give a particularly elegant line when they are made from a light, unlined fabric, such as taffeta or silk.

However, there is nothing static or rigid in the way the draperies fall, because he is most particular about how they are hung and dressed. These are his instructions: "The first thing to do once they are hung is to walk away from the window, holding up the hems. Then let the curtain fall back naturally. Never force the fabric into corrugated folds." This policy is borne out by one of his makers, who says that when he first worked for Roger he was

How to make something out of nothing. Two awkward windows in an attic conversion presented a challenge, met by making an exact template of the shape and then devising fold-up Roman blinds. In a simple bathroom this treatment suffices (opposite, top), but to create a more elaborate setting for a dressing table an Italian-strung dress curtain is added to soften the angles on the window (left). A centrally placed candelabra further enhances the sense of theatricality.

On an inaccessible stair window, a neat ribbon-strung translucent blind that does not need to be pulled down is a good solution (opposite, bottom). Add a border of some kind of banding on all four edges to give the window definition and presence.

conventional dressing. Shades are a handsome answer. There is no point in making a silk purse out of a sow's ear in such a situation. You just have to do the best thing possible, which is to make the simplest possible shade to fit the offending space. Dress the shade with smart tapes or, if the window frame is ugly, disguise it with a simple stationary panel. Roger dislikes draperies that stop at the windowsill, so he sometimes uses a completely flat width of fabric and hangs it from eyelets over cup hooks so that it can be folded back like a sail. In his own kitchen, as a whimsical antidote, he has given up on draperies altogether and instead hangs a transient array of unrelated objects—a wooden hanger, dish towel, picture frame, a single flower. He can find inspiration everywhere. His great friend Fiona Shelburne says they often go to the cinema to see black-and-white movies, for which they share a passion. It is not unusual, however, for the entire audience to be surprised out of their seats when Roger exclaims enthusiastically, "Darling, just look at those wonderful draperies!'

used to dressing draperies very precisely. On their first job together, Roger was horrified by this method; he grabbed the drapery, pulled it away from the window, dropped it and said, "That is how it should be done."

Roger's personal preference is to allow the chintzes he chooses for window treatments to play a secondary role to the star performers. Therefore, a chintz may feature as functional draw draperies behind theatrical stationary panels, or as a flat pull-down shade tucked behind the main draperies. He

is always looking for ways to bend the rules, to use fabrics out of their logical context. This is evident in the way he mixes fabrics of different weight, pattern, and color, so that the traditional arrangement might be reversed, using the chintz as the working draperies and a subtle stripe as the panels, for example.

Generally, Roger prefers printed cotton and linen to silk, but is perfectly happy to produce a concoction of ethereal pleats and ruffles. There are always some windows, however, which, by the nature of their shape, defy

Furnishings
and
Furniture

Grouping *Furniture*

*T*he ability to walk into a room and see what needs to be done to swiftly improve its looks, making it more comfortable for its inhabitants, without the outlay for any elaborate purchases, is an enviable skill. Roger Banks-Pye can set interiors at ease by moving the furniture, and often the objects, to make little conversational groups in the right places, with tables at the right height, with flowers and a pencil, pad and telephone immediately at hand. Grouping furniture is important; people often arrange furniture according to what looks right rather than encouraging people to feel at ease. "How often do we go into a room and find chairs placed so that only one person can sit and talk to himself in a corner, with all the other chairs distanced at the far side of the room? Nobody wants to feel left out so why isolate chairs?" Roger always

Balanced distribution of furniture around a room *ensures that this studio apartment always feels spacious and comfortable, both for daytime use, with its variety of seating possibilities, and when the scroll-ended day bed is made up for the night and the dining chairs are lined up out of the way. The tall wardrobe along one wall hides everyday clutter such as clothes and a television set.*

A great variety of chair types grouped together *to make cozy corners to sit in make a welcoming environment in the drawing room of Roger's London apartment (opposite).*

Despite the fact that he has used exotic and seemingly expensive materials, such as the faux *leopard skin used in blue on the footstool (below) and more natural tones on the nearby chair, Roger manages to create an aura of cozy intimacy and luxurious comfort.*

A beribboned chair, designed to demonstrate an unusual way of using trimmings (right), is poised invitingly near a convenient table.

arranges chairs and sofas and ottomans so that people can move about freely and sit together, whatever the dimensions of a room. It is a luxury to have more than one definite seating group, but he always strives to create them, even if one simply comprises a pair of upright chairs placed at a small table.

Whenever he first walks into any room, Roger considers what he would do if the room were his own. "Sofas and chairs should talk to one another—either tête-à-tête or for a general gossip. Placing a pair of sofas at right

angles to the unlit fire creates a trap for only four people, and should be avoided. I never put a sofa across the window—it is a huge mass that blocks the light. Rather place two chairs in front of the window and they will be silhouetted gracefully, as well as visually opening out the space. After years of trial and error I have found that, whatever the size of the room, one can only get eight people sitting comfortably together other than at a table. Everybody wants to sit by the fire, to have somewhere to put down a drink, and never to feel isolated."

Roger emphatically believes that the only real consideration in every scheme is comfort. "It was vital to Nancy Lancaster, less so to John Fowler who would cover his *chaises-longues* in pale blue silk—they would look wonderful but you slipped off them." If a room looks nervous, people will never be comfortable. Little things convey that nervousness; a lack of ashtrays, or feeling the need to place glasses in an ashtray so as not to leave rings on the table. "I have found that a room looks comfortable when it is," says Roger.

A good plan for furniture positioning *is vital before a decorative scheme goes ahead. This sketch of David and Judy Greens' living room, shown in its finished state overleaf, shows how carefully Roger will plan a room so that everything fits in properly, with room to walk around the chairs. The placement of lighting and those small tables Roger favours, on which he can place a little basket of greenery if need be, is also decided. The details of fabrics may change (checks were, in fact, used to cover the sofas, with floral patterns on the cushions, rather than the reverse shown here), and the decorative objects chosen may differ, but the all-important shapes and position of the furniture are fixed.*

"How often do we go into a room and find chairs placed so that only one person can sit and talk to himself in a corner, all the others distanced at the far side of the room? Nobody wants to feel left out."

The Greens' drawing room is an excellent example of mixing different upholstery in one room. Solids with patterns, linens with velvet and chintz, an armchair in a velvet leopard spot, two sofas in Eaton check weave and two chairs in rust cotton damask: all mingle happily (left). The look is both comfortable and laid back, in a contemporary, unstructured way that is entirely right for the 1990s. Again, maximum use is made of the space for creating different seating groups to give flexible choices. The unusual fireside recess (right) provides ample room for a fireside chair, while on the other side of the room (below) there is a comfortable sofa with a window view and natural light streaming in.

Consider the mix within a room of different pieces of furniture in different fabrics. The shape of upholstery is also important, especially when the back of a chair or sofa is prominent within the room. Roger generally chooses classic, old shapes for upholstery, since they inspire a feeling of confidence and comfort. It is important to be aware of the height of the arms and back and the depth of the seats, since nothing looks worse than a big man perched on a tiny little rose-covered chair or a woman on a sofa with her feet six

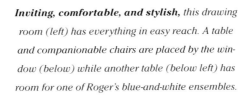

Inviting, comfortable, and stylish, this drawing room (left) has everything in easy reach. A table and companionable chairs are placed by the window (below) while another table (below left) has room for one of Roger's blue-and-white ensembles.

The shape of of furniture is vital for dictating how conversational groups are arranged. A high-backed box shape (above) provides privacy and so is is ideal for conspiratorial chats for two, while a back-to-back chair can be used to link two quite separate groups.

inches above floor level. A curved-back chair looks more welcoming than an upright straight-backed chair.

Every seat should have a table beside it, Roger believes, and there should be some 28-inch table heights as well as coffee tables. "Proper height tables give authority and dignity to a room. Square topped or round, stacking tables in dark or light wood, whatever, dot them around and keep the surfaces clear enough so that you can put down a tray where you want."

Chairs

"There are no rules," advises Roger, when discussing the possible alternatives for covering the seats on a set of chairs. "Upholster furniture with fabric that suits its shape and style and, finally, to suit the scheme of the room. A delicate little gilt wood chair would look wonderful finished in black leather with black studs." The chairs on this page illustrate his point. Although they are very different in shape, period and color, both types of chair look immaculate in their broad toffee-colored check, whose scale suits their individual proportions. Both chairs are space-nailed over braid to present a defined line to the upholstery. Roger generally prefers to use space-nailing instead of close-nailing because it gives a less severe finish. Traditionally, space-nailing would only be done on heavier fabrics, such as damask, leather and needlepoint, but that does not preclude Roger's using it on a much wider range of fabrics.

He doesn't see chairs simply as practical or comfortable things to sit on; his graphic eye turns them into decorative objects in their own right, and he is always conscious that the outline of a chair should make a contribution to its setting. Chairs do not always have to be taken very

***Dissimilar chairs can look equally well dressed** in the same fabric. Smart beige-and-white checked weave works on reproduction 19th-century dining chairs (left and above), acting as a foil to the dark wood, or on more delicate Louis XVI chairs, with a design to match the checked pattern, newly painted on the cane backs (right). What is vital is the finish: both are trimmed with a smart line of space-nailing over contrasting braid.*

upholstered dining chair is dressed in a practical slipcover of the same fabric so that it can be changed when necessary.

Most of the upholstered chairs Roger uses are ones whose form and structure have been perfected by Colefax and Fowler over the years. Roger has a deep understanding of the fabrics he is dealing with, from construction to trimmings; and his sketches reveal a great enthusiasm for developing new ideas. His upholstery designs are utterly sumptuous; but, although comfort is paramount, it is his attention to detail that lifts them above

the standard. Where someone else might be content to add a deep bullion fringe to the base of a chair, Roger will add another, smaller fringe over the top. He always contrast-binds the edges of chair skirts and ruffles but he uses chintz reversed so it has a softer, faded finish. Instead of using the standard width of piping, he will use an extra narrow one in an unusual way—winding it up an upholstered arm, perhaps. No detail is overlooked: having covered a mahogany chair in tartan, he hand-painted the piping so that it matched the lines within the fabric.

*Chairs can be fun, **not just functional.** The kitchen chair (far left) has a practical washable vinyl seat, but the stripes are continued on the back and down the legs, so that the curves of the chair are reduced to almost a shadowy form. The rush-seated chair has a charming French country look helped by two-toned paint, and the slipcover on the dining chair is made from dust sheets. Another checked slip covers a round-seated woven chair in Roger's apartment (above)*

Used as part of a tableau, this line-up of farmhouse chairs has been deliberately placed to form a decorative feature in its own right. The checked cotton cushion covers echo the samples of American homespun fabric in the frames above.

seriously—as is evident from the photographs on these pages. The seat of the striped kitchen chair has been covered in vinyl so that it can be wiped down after muddy hunters have had their lunch. Roger painted on stripes running down its length, ignoring the rise and fall of its contours. The rush-seated country chairs are painted in shades of yellow, similar to the way in which Roger paints doors different shades of the same color. The seats are usually covered with simple flat squabs of gingham check and the

*"A good chair
should look as if
it could spring at you
or take you
in its arms."*

More than any other item of furniture, *a chair can appear to have its own character. In his sketches Roger loves to explore unusual treatments to accentuate this. Some of his designs go on to be made up, others remain as delightful ideas on the page which might one day be realized (above left). Each chair is designed to maximize its individual personality, while always being put in the context of its surroundings and use. Roger employs an enormous variety of detail in his finishing: fringes, skirts, tufting, braiding and piping all contribute to the final immaculate effect. Never content with the standard, he will use a trellis fringe at skirt-length (top left), or even two fringes overlapping (above, left, and right).*

The handling of fine detail can be the making of fine upholstered furniture. Here, ultra-thin tricolored piping cord is used to bind the arm of a damask-covered chair (left). It serves not only to highlight the smooth curves of the arm but also to introduce a subtle touch of yellow which picks up colors used elsewhere in the room.

An unusual French antique chair with wraparound wings is neatly dressed in a tough upholstery fabric with a delicate sprigged design (below). Space-nailing over braid accentuates the beautiful lines of the chair. Each individual panel of the chair—back, front, and sides—and even the small padded armrests (above) has been given the same painstaking treatment.

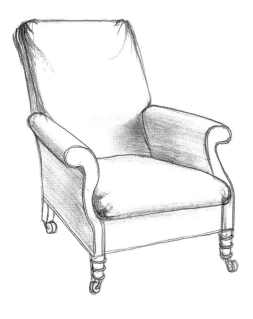

"I generally choose classic, old shapes for upholstery—they inspire a feeling of comfort and confidence."

How welcoming and comforting a deep, well-sprung easy chair is, and what a variety of styles and coverings can be found to suit everyone's requirements. Comfort is paramount, of course. The shape should be such that you can sink down unhindered, but there should be adequate support for your arms and back. A wing chair (below) offers a degree of privacy, hence its traditional use in libraries and studies. But the large surface area that an easy chair offers within a decorative scheme needs careful consideration too. Colors and fabrics can be chosen either to blend in or to make a feature of the chair. A red chair (right) lends a dash of fire to an otherwise cool and muted color scheme, while the floral fabric (opposite) has been used inside out to give it a softer look.

Gannochy Lodge

SLIP COVERS
FOR THE LEATHER
GAINSBOROUGH
CHAIRS.

NO PIPING
BUT THE PLEATS
OF THE SKIRTS
LINED BLUE

THE BASE OF
THE SKIRTS FINISHED
ON A BLUE LINE

Cool blues and American homespuns *cover the chairs in this living room.*
The fireside chairs designed by Roger, resembling a sofa sawn in two and
divided by the fire, have proved to be a highly popular and versatile design,
allowing proximity to the fire without unbalancing the distribution of furniture.

Gannochy Lodge

THE PURE DOWN
CUSHION IN GANNOCHY
TOILE THE WRONG WAY ROUND
SELF PIPED

SPACED
No 9
BRONZE
NAILING

CONTRAST PIPED
DARKER OTTOMAN

*The Carnegie
fireside chair*

"Always consider the shape of the piece of furniture and the other furniture in the room before you choose the upholstery fabric," is Roger's advice. One of his favorite ploys to enhance the shape is to layer fabrics over each other: a broad border of patterned fabric over the back and seat of a chair, for example, or an appliquéd spray of chintz flowers blanket stitched to the base material. He will even use a fabric turned inside out, as he did with a 1950s floral cretonne which has been used the wrong way around to cover a sofa and chair. The reversed fabric, muted and softened, gives a delightfully abstract look, like a watercolor painting. In the same room, a deeply comfortable armchair is covered in scarlet "Tree of Life" linen. Together, these chairs give a contrasting kick to the sea of blue elsewhere in the room and prevent it from being too contrived and passive.

Roger delights in using old fabric designs from the Colefax and Fowler archives, and on occasion, has himself made a contribution to the accuracy of the historical records. Some time ago, when he was working with Fiona Shelburne on the decoration of her home, Bowood House, they found a mass of old slipcovers lying in trunks in the barns. Long ago discarded from the house, the covers were in perfect condition. Designer and client rushed around the house, covering every piece of furniture they could with them. A "Bowood" fabric had already been reproduced as a document print, but the old sample's greens had faded to blue. Now Roger was able to return happily to London with an unfaded cover; and the true colorway was produced for the company's 60th anniversary.

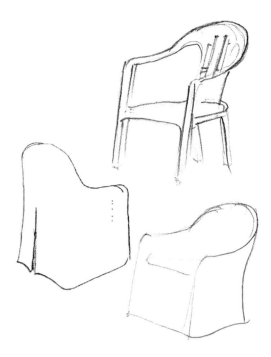

Roger has been designing chair covers since his days styling shop windows for Colefax and Fowler. With his couturier's eye for fabric and the way it hangs and falls, he will dress chairs as he would a human model, the fabric draped to flatter pleasing curves, such as the narrow "waist" of dressingtable chairs (center left), or used to disguise less than perfect features, such as an ill-proportioned, clumsy leg.

Making something new and amusing out of a standard article is a challenge Roger loves. The distinctly unstylish plastic garden chairs sketched above, which can be bought in any hardware store, metamorphose into something eyecatching and witty in their dashing slipcovers (right).

Cushions
and Pillows

The creation of beautifully tailored cushions has become one of Roger's signatures. He has had years of experience designing cushions for shop windows, exhibitions, and advertising shoots, as well as for customers. Today he still manages to find smart and amusing ways of making them. Cushions are a useful method of introducing a decorative leitmotif while adding to personal comfort and contributing to the room's decorative geometry. Certainly, some of Roger's designs are very complicated and costly, but many of these ideas can be adapted to suit the resources and skills available.

One principal requirement is to make sure that every cushion, bolster, or pillow always looks well fed; there is nothing worse than ending up with a pizza-style cushion squashed into the corner of a sofa or being jabbed in the lower back by a fistful of congealed filling. Three factors ensure that this doesn't happen. Firstly, the pad stuffing has to be the right combination of feather and down. Down is softer and lighter but doesn't hold its shape well; feather gives a firmer structure but needs looking after by being frequently fluffed up. Secondly, the size of the pillow form must be at least two inches larger than the

The perfect tailoring of cushions is of great importance to Roger, and he was so impressed and influenced by John Stephanidis's cushion (left), which has a chic picot braid pattern, that it is included here as a fine example of discreet sophistication. A similar black design was appliquéd on a boldly colored background on a scallop-edged cushion (right and above) to make a good foil for the strong lines of a striped and nailed upholstered chair.

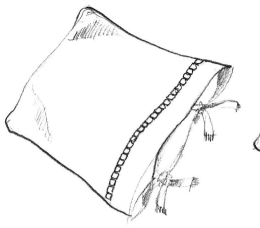

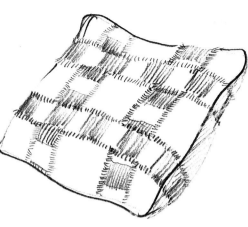

Drawnthread work and simple ties *adorn Roger's slipcover cushion design.*

Frayed bands of fabric *applied in a checkerboard design make an unusual effect.*

Two decoy ducks in a panel *perch on waves of blue stripes finished with cord piping.*

Contrasts of cushion fabric *seen against different chair materials magnify their decorative appeal.*

finished size of its cover. (Size is important; Roger sometimes uses anything from a 20-inch case to a 24-inch case for a big sofa or a day bed.) The third rule is to treat the cushions with as much respect as you would a work of art!

Such perfectionism goes hand in hand with the attention he gives to the precise concoction of his cushion designs. There is nothing haphazard about his choice of fabrics and trimmings, but there is always enormous scope for variation. One of his favored devices is to use appliqué in some form, and one of the simplest ways is to cut out a panel and "frame" it within another fabric. Another method is to blanket stitch cut-out shapes and panels onto the base material. Roger often uses strips of contrasting material such as the diagonally cut straps of material he applied to some gingham cushions in his London bedroom, or fabric stripes with frayed edges, as in his sketch. Details are just as important as they would be on a pair of draperies or on furniture upholstery.

Roger loves to experiment with every sort of fan edging, cord, and piping, but will always make sure his choice relates to the style of cushion and the way it works in its given situation. In Trudi Ballard's studio, for example, the day bed is strewn with huge pillows finished with a wide ruffle—a practical and feminine touch in this structured monochrome environment. He also likes to use real

Roger uses unusually narrow piping to finish his shaped seat squabs (left) and chair cushions (right). He has even been known to paint in fine details on the piping by hand so that the pattern line is uninterrupted.

bed pillows on sofas sometimes, having been influenced by the huge white pillows found on the dark green leather Chesterfield sofas at Brooks' Club in London.

Roger tells a story about his initiation by John Fowler into the ritual of Arranging the Cushions. "There is an art to plumping up cushions which I practise to this day: hold the top corners, shake down, let go, never squash flat or you break the spines of the feathers. I learned this in the garden room at John Fowler's home, the Hunting Lodge. I dutifully followed the ritual and then placed the plain white silk cushions on the blue sofa but, to my astonishment, he said, 'No, silly! You've put them the wrong way round.' 'But they're plain white,' I replied. 'Yes, and the weave must always go from east to west, not from north to south!'" This is done, Roger explains, to catch the light on the surface of the fabric to highlight the subtleties of texture and color. The lesson must have had some effect, because Roger has observed this rule ever since. He is equally insistent that cushions should never be perched on their corners as if in an uncomfortable balancing act.

Cushions can be used to great effect to add a note of contrast to whatever else is happening in the room, or indeed as a device to draw the whole scheme together—picking up a note of color in the drapery fabric, for example, or even using the same design of fabric. A cushion can contribute not only in terms of color, but sometimes also in texture, serving as a foil to its "host" sofa or chair; velvet on tweed: needlepoint on check, leopard spot on chintz, check on bouclé . . . imagination is the only limitation.

Cushions add to the overall feeling of comfort in a room, being both visually pleasing and physically inviting. They should always be the correct size and look at home in their given situation. Roger is very particular about how they are placed—he hates to see cushions balanced on one of their corners because it spoils the line. He often uses European square pillows (opposite), particularly on day beds and Chesterfield sofas.

The relationship between cushion and 'host' is very important. A contrast of materials can make for an interesting tension. A smart toffee-colored checked cushion (below) sits on a leopard-spot velvet-covered chair.

"Pure down is an absolute luxury to be enjoyed. It does require constant attention to keep its shape but it is worth it."

Beds
and
Bed Dressing

A four-poster bed in the 17th or 18th century was the most treasured and costly item in the household, and the craftsmanship that went into the carving of its frame and the richness of its draperies reflected the prestige and pride of the family who owned it. Today, even if we don't judge the bed's owner by the same standards, a grand bed certainly makes a magnificent contribution to the style and comfort of a bedroom. Roger's view of what makes a really good bed, above all other decorative considerations, is that comfort is paramount, and that doesn't just mean the quality of the mattress. Nevertheless, he would be perfectly happy to have made the finest, most expensive white

A cool, pristine haven is created by the all-white dressing of Valentino's bed, with its classic sun-ray canopy, and linen and lace draperies, which are brought into sharp contrast by the rich coloring of the rest of the decoration.

horsehair mattress if it was a particular requirement for a client. He thinks that all modern beds are too low to be truly accommodating; a bed should be at a height where you can prop yourself up in bed and socialize with someone sitting on a chair nearby without having to squint up at them. You should be able to look out at the view, if you have one, rather than just a slice of sky. You must be able to reach out to your bedside table without the blood draining from your arm.

As to size in relation to the scale of the room, he feels that generous twin beds are easier to deal with decoratively because they look good in any room, but he concedes that since most people don't want twin beds for their principal rooms, the bed must suit the needs of its incumbent. Valentino's 18th-century bed—which belonged to Lord Kitchener in the early 1900s—is immense in relation to the bedroom's proportions, but it perfectly suits the richness and density of the decoration.

True to Roger's statement that "canopies and coronets can make the bed as elaborate as a room within a room," the bed has been deliberately dressed to maximize its sense of isolation from the rest of the room. The entire interior gives an aura of tranquillity, with its fine white linen bed curtains and valance and its cotton and lace pillows, sheets, and cover.

The beds in Roger's London home are the antithesis of such grandeur, but just as welcoming. His own bed is an elegant early

"*Choose beds for comfort and for looks. Like modern sofas, most modern beds are too low. You should have to climb into a bed not drop onto it. Antique beds are just the right height.*"

19th-century bird's-eye maple sleigh bed on which he uses a homey mixture of blue-and-white bedclothes, cushions and pillowcases. Likewise, the day bed that sits under the window in his living room has a blue-and-white theme. As this is a simple iron bedstead, Roger has wittily created the illusion of "the pauper's palliasse" and covered the bed in a stylized frayed-edged patchwork bedspread made for him by a friend. His preferred bed shape has a proper headboard and footboard of equal heights, which he thinks gives a finished look. Apart from these criteria its provenance and style is unimportant; it could be a sleigh bed or equally well have upholstered scroll ends, for example.

Roger's own homes have always been a testing ground for his decorating experiments, and they are full of innovation and wit. The warm tones of his blonde wood sleigh bed make a good partner for an assortment of blue-and-white bed linen, propounding the Swedish look (opposite).

A Victorian iron bedstead sits under the window in the living room, posing as a chaise longue. Covered in a frayed patchwork quilt made from dishrags and dusters by a friend of Roger's, it adds to the story of "shabby chic" (right and above).

Two deliciously feminine bed treatments in traditional style—but with subtle differences. Despite his preference for white bed dressings, Roger has, for these particular treatments, conceded a minutely patterned voile for the interior draperies (opposite and below) to complement the chintz outer draperies. However he has been loyal to his usual pure white for the bedspreads : white taffeta is diagonally quilted in double lines of red silk (see detail, opposite).

The finishing details are suitably generous to do justice to such grand and imposing beds. A traditional gathered valance is given enormous strength by the addition of a bound upstand, or rosette, rope, and soft triple goblets at each corner (left and below). An excessive gathered fringe exaggerates the curved shape of the wooden canopy. The trimmings on both of these bed treatments relate to the window drapery finishes in the room.

Since most beds occupy the largest amount of space in a bedroom and are the central purpose of the room, the way they are to be dressed is vital to the overall scheme. Grand four-poster beds are obvious candidates for dressing in a traditionally magnificent style, but any type of bed can be adorned with additional dressings and structures to add gravitas. A classic treatment with an elegantly draped corona above the bed can give a fluid vertical line that balances the bed mass in relation to the proportions of the curtains. Bed draperies made from the same chintz as the window draperies ensure that the decorative harmony is not lost. As with all draperies, particular regard is paid to getting the proportions right to balance the whole effect, as well as giving attention to the finest details of finishing. Usually, Roger likes to see the bed interior finished entirely in plain white fabric, ideally linen, but in some situations he will use a pretty voile with a tiny motif.

Where possible, of course, Roger prefers to experiment with alternative fabrics, as the story told by a businessman client illustrates. For a tiny bedroom, furnished with a few pieces of elegant Russian and Charles X furniture, Roger had wanted to produce a sable bedcover. The client demurred. "In reading the estimate, I noticed that among the costs for nails, wallpaper, fabric and the like, there was a passing reference to a bedspread to be made from 'fur with a scarlet lining.' My middle-class prejudices were disturbed by this and I telephoned Roger, who obviously had had hopes that I would miss it. He said that he supposed I would prefer beige taffeta, which sounded fine to me. From his tone of voice I should have known that he was not going to take this piece of 'philistinism' lying down. Sure enough, in strict conformity with our discussion, the beige taffeta item was placed on the bed. It was only later, when it was turned back that the brothel-red lining was revealed in all its glory. I confess that originally I though it garish but my eye has been educated by Roger and it now looks entirely and obviously appropriate."

A prettily draped corona anchors the large bed to the wall and balances its scale in relation to the floor-length window draperies (opposite, top). The bedspread is double-stitched for geometric emphasis, instead of the more traditional outline quilting (opposite, below).

In such a richly patterned bedroom (above) something special had to be put on the bed. The client rejected fur, so Roger provided a luxurious silk velvet and taffeta bedspread (right), which is so heavy it takes two people to remove it.

He prefers to have relatively plain bedcovers as a contrast to the many yards of patterned fabric he employs on the outside of the bed and elsewhere. A favored embellishment, whether the fabric is patterned or solid-colored, is to employ cross quilting, sometimes with double rows of stitching for emphasis. He employs this technique, rather than the traditional method of outline quilting, because he considers that this method results in a fussy effect he wishes to avoid.

$S\,c\,r\,e\,e\,n\,s$

Screens have been in widespread use since the 15th century or longer. Down the centuries, they have warded off drafts and excessive heat from open fires, hidden entrances and exits, and protected modesty. They have been fashioned from wood and leather, needlepoint and paper, the finest lacquerwork, and delicately painted canvas. But to suit today's interiors, screens don't have to exist for a purely practical purpose. We live in such a controlled environment nowadays, with few unwelcome drafts and extremes of heat to spoil the complexion, that screens may be allowed to play a more aesthetic role.

There is something about a screen that is very come-hitherish and it is a fine way of creating an element of surprise—the onlooker can't help being curious to know what goes on behind it! For example, a screen can make a partial division between rooms without the visual finality of a door, and, at the same time, give a teasing sense of speculation as to what lies beyond. Conversely, one might be used in front of a door as an additional, more decorative barrier. Roger has done this at his country house in a small double-bedded guest room in which the

Used as a barrier, a screen can give an impression of coziness and privacy, or it can be used to visually change the proportion of a room. The decoration can be varied on the two sides (right) to suit the facing view.

Screens can be purely decorative, a canvas on which to explore fine detailing (above). A linear backdrop draws attention to the column and the canvas-and-leather "urn" (opposite) to make an amusing vignette. The panels of the screen echo the panels of the door, so that it becomes an architectural extension of it.

screened door adds to the aura of cozy privacy: when someone enters the room, they do so without instantly invading the occupant's personal space . In a beautifully decorated, large house in Scotland he has placed a screen in front of the door that leads from the dining room to the kitchen for both aesthetic and practical reasons: it forms a barrier between the food preparation area and the area where guests are entertained. A screen can also be a practical alternative for window treatments. Where daylight is at a premium—at a small window, for example—a screen could be a substitute for draperies, using pleated material within a simple frame, perhaps.

Roger includes screens to give height to a room where he has not wanted to use the more usual devices of, for example, striped wall finishes or vertically displayed decorative objects and pictures. Employed in this way, the screen becomes a design statement in its own right and must therefore have excellent structure and detailed finishing. Whatever the screen is made from or covered in, the size and design should suit its given situation. A *faux* paneled screen looks lean and masculine, while one upholstered in material and finished with gimp may have softer, feminine lines. A screen can be utterly plain, with strong, straight lines to its frame, or flamboyantly curvaceous and painted. Also, the two sides of a solid screen don't have to present the same design, so they could show a different face depending on the vantage point, which all adds to the fun. The screens Roger uses are always ultra-smart, and the upholstered ones are finished with the same precise detail that any upholstered chair of his design would be.

A screen makes a strong linear backdrop and frame for a still-life arrangement or where some special object needs attention focused on it. In his own house, Roger has created a wonderfully theatrical scene using a screen and a column with a humorous "urn" on top. Each object benefits from the presence of the other and the whole makes an amusing statement as one leaves the room.

A generously proportioned screen with wide panels is substantial enough to act as a sturdy room divider, creating a corridor between kitchen and dining room to separate the eating and working areas. The smart graphic check accentuates the structure of the screen while acting as a counter-balance to the asymmetrical arrangement of pictures to one side of the door. The vertical thrust that any screen naturally provides in a room is further emphasized here by the placing of three plates above the doorway to lead the eye above and beyond the normal sight level.

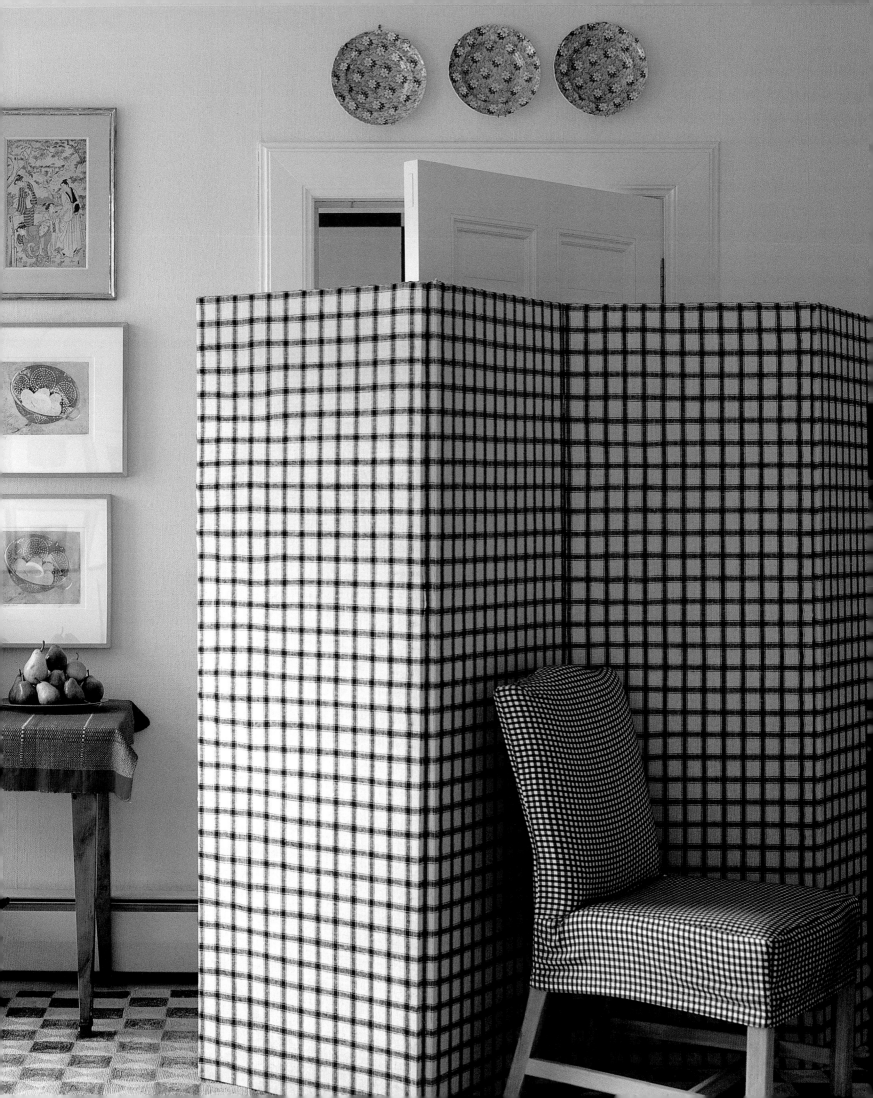

$\mathcal{L}ight$
and
$\mathcal{H}eat$

$\mathcal{T}$he way rooms are lit affects their atmosphere. One of the reasons why an interior designed by Roger Banks-Pye always appears welcoming is because of the way he lights it. This is all the more inspiring when you consider how simply he does it, relying mainly upon table lamps with the occasional swing-arm extendable wall or floor light to provide pools of light where needed. There are no star-burst ceilings of low-voltage lights with in-built transformers, only a few wall sconces to cast light up, and certainly no fluorescent-tubed downlighters hidden behind baffles, which is the way architects are prone to light interiors.

So how does he manage to light rooms so simply but effectively? Firstly, he uses a great many lamps—as many as eight in a small living room is normal to Roger. Secondly, he positions them very carefully. Because he likes to have conversational groups of chairs and sofas, with occasional tables next to them, he groups the furniture first and then positions the lights. Finally, he controls the quality of the light. He uses ordinary incandescent bulbs, but by carefully selecting shades for their reflective qualities as well as their decorative appearance, he is able to manipulate the way the light is emitted.

__The traditional concept of reflected light and heat__ is here turned on its head. A mirror asymmetrically positioned over a dummy fireplace reflects light from a ceiling candelabra and from two French whitewashed wooden candlesticks with bound parchment shades which have been grouped together rather than stood at either end of the mantel. Together with old creamware dishes, the whole scene contributes to the stylized cream-and-drab color scheme.

"Any room, whatever its size, looks better with many little pools of light rather than a general glare. I like intimate low light just where and when you need it."

Lamps with traditional shades, open at the top and bottom, emit two-directional light. Roger either warms up that light to a golden glow by lining the shade with gold paper or cools it with a silver lining. Shades are important since you see them dotted around the room in daylight, so their effect when the light is switched off should be considered. Dead lamps always look sad, and white shades, in particular, can look like hatboxes. Dark shades work better on unlit lamps and dark heavy paper shades lined with gold give a room instant glamour. It is important to mix shades—have some opaque paper, some pleated silk, and some simply cream translucent paper.

Decorators generally prefer table lamps to more architectural built-in lighting systems because they furnish the tables next to chairs, sofas, and beds. But only the skillful avoid trails of cord behind furniture or coiling from tables. Roger always conceals the power source of the light. There are no bundles of cords and there is always a switch at hand—a simple point but one that is too often over-

Using an extensive variety of lamps and shades means that great play can be made with them as part of the decorative battery. Wherever they are placed, on a bedside table or a desk, they form part of a tableau with other objects, both ornamental, such as flowers, or practical, such as a telephone or pencil pot.

It is a prerequisite of Roger's lighting arrangements that a lamp should be within easy reach and that the balance of light should be maintained whatever the room's proportions or the time of day. A room full of visual distractions such as a picture-lined library (right) needs substantial shades and bases that will not get lost in the general confusion.

looked. More often than not, Roger paints the flat of the baseboards off-black, including the outlets, and then finally the lamp plugs. In a room where the baseboards are *faux* stone the electricity sockets have been painted in the same effect, which makes for a seamless transition.

This constant attention to such details ensures the comfort of whoever is going to use the room. Nowhere is this better demonstrated than in a bedroom in which the four-poster bed is dressed in rich draperies. Ingeniously, Roger wired a pair of extendable-arm brass reading lights inside the curtains so that the occupant of the bed does not have to draw back the cozy drapes in order to read, and the switch can be found quickly and easily without having to grope around among the folds of the fabric. To back up these lights there are two hanging lamps, one shaded with paper and the other pleated, so that wherever you sit in this comfortable room—beside the fire, at the desk near the window, or in the upholstered chair, you have light at hand. It is only when you inhabit the space

that you can appreciate Roger's considerable skill at casting light exactly where you need it. Modernists, who believe that bathing a room with a uniform white light suggests clarity and spaciousness, might be interested to see the effect achieved in a box-like apartment block of the 1930s, with only one modest window in the living room. The flat is used only at night, so Roger devised a scheme for creating pools of light that made the optimum use of shadows as contrast. The lighting consists of green tole urn lamps with white silk shades

and a floor lamp angled over the desk, with six other lamps carefully placed around the room. Traditional picture lights hang over the portraits on the walls. This arrangement makes the small room appear larger, the shadows disguising its true extent, and at the same time more cozy. The pools of concentrated light absorb colors such as the deep red and green of the walls and furnishings.

Daylight is as important as artificial light in a Banks-Pye interior. It determines where he places a desk in a room, so that the

occupant does not work in his/her own shadow, or where he hangs a mirror, to reflect as much light as possible. Just as the quality of light varies during the course of the day between bright sunshine and twilight, the difference in intensity of light and depth of shadow is controlled and emphasized. When there are no good windows, in a basement room perhaps, Roger intensifies the color on big surface areas and creates pools of light in the room, giving it an air of mystery. The only overhead light source he uses is the natural light of a skylight or a chandelier, never too large or too branched. The chandelier must fit the space it is designed to illuminate, whether it is a narrow hallway or a large dining room, in which case it must not dwarf the table top— or the diners.

Roger Banks-Pye understands the way in which light can alter the entire mood of a room. In his own London living room, he has re-created the mellow glow of Venetian afternoons, drawing the light from north and south through small leaded windows, burnishing the walls to a soft glow with gesso. Well-placed mirrors bounce back the light from

Light, warmth, and comfort come together in Roger's country drawing room (left) with wall sconces, table lamps, and reflections from the mirror and fire. "I felt the room should be cozy, warm and rather shabby," says Roger unashamedly.

Minimal lamplight and a roaring fire provide moody lighting for a dark-paneled room lined with books (below).

the windows in summer and from the flickering firelight in winter. He even hangs mirror upon mirror above the fireplace, a device borrowed from the early 19th-century architect Sir John Soane. Soane has been an influence throughout Roger's career, and the Soane house and museum at Lincoln's Inn Fields in London has been an inspiration to him. "Sir John Soane's museum is the place to learn about the effect mirrors can have with natural light, to achieve those magical little illuminating flashes," Roger maintains. Soane designed the house where he lived from 1813 to 1837 as a setting for his antiquities and works of art. The breakfast parlor has a shallow dome for indirect overhead lighting and a variety of mirrors to bounce back all reflected light. This room, with its vista across the yard, is where Soane felt that he captured "the poetry of architecture."

Glass panels around a skylight is just one Soane idea adopted by Roger Banks-Pye. He frequently uses mirrors in unexpected places to open up a feeling of space. Inside the hall door of his own London apartment, mirrored door panels reflect the light from the open doorway, visually doubling the width of his narrow hall. Above the doorway leading from a dressing room into a connecting bathroom in another house he inserted narrow mirror panels up to the ceiling. When asked why he had bothered to put mirrors at such a height, where no one could see in them to use them, Roger replied that they were there so that "giraffes can check their eyelashes." It was a typically amusing response which belies the serious purpose behind the positioning of the mirrors. They are, in fact, perfectly designed to optimize the light from the single window in a long dark room, and they are entirely appropriate to the view of the bathroom beyond. On each side of a large mullioned window in the same house, Roger placed a long rectangular Regency mirror in a gold frame with a candlestick beneath each. They give off flashes of light which are reflected over in the leaded panes of the windows.

Bathroom lighting can be particularly difficult. It needs to illuminate well without being unkind, and yet it should be adaptable enough to allow soothing ambient light when required. Extendable walls lights (right) are an attractive option which offers obliging flexibility.

Using mirrors to bounce back reflected light from windows or conveniently placed lamps (left) boosts low light levels. For the same reason, window treatments should be simple. such as a pull-down shade (above).

Pulling up a chair around the fire in winter is one of the pleasures of life, but not every *pied-à-terre* in the inner city has a fireplace. If it does not, and the rooms are high-ceilinged and spacious, Roger designs one to act as a focal point for the room. He always makes sure the fireplace facing has an understated elegance; dressing it carefully on either side, and arranging amusing objects on and around it, such as a parrot or an obelisk, a whimsical picture of saintly pilgrims, or fruit in a jardinière on the mantelshelf. As was customary in 18th-century France, Roger usually fixes a mirror above the mantel. However, he sometimes chooses to avoid the predictable combination of a mirror in the center and a pair of objects placed on either side. He will position the mirror off center, or add an extra mirror or a clock hung from an old chain or cord. "Sometimes it is better to stand a pair of objects together on the shelf," he says.

Everyone prefers to see a roaring fire rather than a dead and empty fireplace, but most people do not take the trouble to light one just to enjoy the effect of the flames. Roger Banks-Pye will: even in summer he will have a fire burning in the grate, extravagantly throwing open the windows to disperse the heat if necessary.

***Light and shade accentuate the architectural detailing** in this Arts and Crafts movement house (right). Shadows play a vital role in highlighting the outlines of the plate shelf, while natural light from the small side window in the fireplace alcove falls onto the pictures. Maximum light in the rest of the room is maintained by keeping the draperies well away from the window, while the fall of electric light is controlled by carefully placing tall floor lamps near the seating area.*

Decorative
Details

Display

*I*magine that you are walking into a newly decorated room where the principal decorative elements have been dealt with. Pristine Brussels-weave carpet, elegant wall and paint finishes, glorious drapery treatment, sumptuous plump sofas and chairs are all in place. But it is still a room without a personality, a sad, dull thing dressed in pretty clothes. The truly finished look of a room, full of all those details that make up the persona and patina of the piece, is quite taken for granted when we enter someone's home. So much so that we don't immediately take in the intricate detail and yet would be horrified by the nakedness if all those comforting bits and pieces weren't there.

Roger is tireless in his quest for perfection when arranging pictures, decorative objects, flowers and *objets trouvés*. He has a circumspect and quick eye when assessing how and where things should be placed and ordered. He can even be quite ruthless in his discrimination and will remove, demote, and displace objects for the sake of the final effect. He also has a very good visual memory and will suddenly rush to the attic to retrieve a particular dusty artefact he recalls if he considers it just right for the arrangement he has in mind. All is guided by an

When putting together items for display, *do some lateral thinking and you will find unexpected and amusing combinations. Examples here are a harmonic group of stony textures of a creamware plate, a drabware vase, an antique gelatin mold, and an ostrich egg (left); painted and lacquered balls on brass candlesticks (above); and a time-worn dish filled with a selection of items Roger borrowed from the kitchen for their contrasting textures – smooth eggs, furry kiwi fruit, papery garlic bulbs – punctuated with spiky pine cones (right).*

"Visually striking rooms can still irritate because of the lack of attention to comforting detail."

overriding sense that everything must contribute to the true comfort and sense of wellbeing in a room—this is not just an illusion. Quite apart from placing the basic necessities of life according to Roger—such as the ever-present ashtray and matches easily to hand—he seeks to arrange things so that the eye glides from one harmonic group to another and is always charmed or amused.

This is by no means as easy as his results would suggest. Everyone manages to accumulate an enormous amount of extra "ornamental baggage" in their lives: sentimental trinkets, Uncle George's hideous carriage clock, impulse buys, a dynasty of family photographs in a wild assortment of frames (Roger thinks photographs of people are very

Roger regards books as beautiful objects in *their own right as well as providers of knowledge. Two alternative uses are to make them part of the display: propped open at something interesting to catch the eye of the passer-by (far left) and piled up as small plinths to manipulate height and color on a side table (left).*

Silver, glass, and pewter must be well *polished if they are to be put on display: either in severely minimalist style (above left) or softened with delicate flowers (above).*

A flower-filled urn provides a focus for this spectacular blue-and-white scene (below).

difficult to combine effectively). Choices need to be made about what stays and what gets relegated. The criterion has nothing to do with how costly something is but everything to do with its graphic quality, use, and wit, so that the simplest objects have as much merit as a priceless heirloom. Roger's years of window-dressing gave him a grounding that results in an enjoyment of using objects in a relaxed, throwaway manner. He admits, however, that he may do so freely in his own homes but is inevitably more circumspect when dealing with clients. At his home in the country he mixes bargain-basement modern porcelain with inherited treasures and then fills the gaps between with trinkets of his own creation. He covers matchboxes in checked fabrics and places them with as much care as he would proffer a Fabergé egg. Scent is another vital component: smoking joss sticks are constantly present to sweeten the air and Roger will always have some on hand, standing in a jar.

But whatever scheme he is working on, he uses the simplest ingredients with humor and imagination. In Trudi Ballard's apartment he has filled a creamware terrine with eggs, garlic, pine cones, and kiwi fruit: literally "throwaway style," but they also add color, pattern, and texture to their setting on the pristine plain mantelpiece below a gloriously ornate Rococo-style mirror frame. The ingredients he uses in his displays always work in harmony together. For instance, he uses different kinds of glass in one group, or echoes the proportions of a tall table lamp by placing a simple long-stemmed flower beside it, or makes a miniature scene of blue-and-white

objects. Whatever is to hand, he will find some way of using it well. He has even adopted musical instruments as a decorative device when they are appropriate to the interests of the owner of the house, placing them on top of the bookshelves as one would a vase or ginger jar.

In another situation he uses books upended on their spines and propped open on tables to reveal an interesting print or display a passage that will amuse. Books are

Always one to fill a basket with something amusing, Roger displays an African studded leather basket holding a rustic twig ball (above), while on a side table he has placed an eclectic array of objects, including an old Bakelite telephone (right). He hates modern phones and fire extinguishers, which have to be hidden in baskets.

nearly always shown minus their dust jackets—Roger dislikes the inevitable shabbiness of thumbed covers. In their undressed state, he can take advantage of their smart solid colors, piling them up as mini-plinths with pretty objects or little pots of flowers on top; a useful way of allowing changes of height. Roger's mission is to dissuade clients from keeping

paperbacks on shiny white shelves behind unlovely objects propped awkwardly on the edge. He would rather see books as decorative objects in their own right, carefully regimented within dark-painted shelves. They might even be allowed to overflow in stacks onto the seat of a chair—so long as they are worthily aesthetic tomes, of course.

Where and how ornaments are displayed affects the proportion and presentation of a room. For example, the exaggerated sense of height given by the striped paper from baseboard to ceiling in the drawing room at his country house has been increased by the vertical emphasis of ornamental display. The eye is drawn upwards with pictures, light sconces, brackets and china arranged in straight lines that finish under the cornice. The effect balances the horizontal weight of decoration in this lushly decked-out room. But Roger stresses that display doesn't have to be permanent. In the hall of a Scottish house, he has arranged a purely theatrical set piece. A slatted garden seat and an upholstered 18th-century sofa flank a classical urn, out of which erupts an explosion of flowers. Beneath, like seeds fallen from the flowers, lies a collection of blue-and-white painted balls, and, to remind us that this is a hall, two sturdy walking sticks complete the picture.

There is a story that tells of Roger going on holiday that illustrates his constant urge to rearrange a room. The moment he arrived in his hotel room, he felt compelled to move the furniture into a more comfortable position, fill the wastebasket with freshly picked greenery, and throw down a cotton rug he had just bought in a local market.

P i c t u r e s

ℛoger has positive views when he is discussing the merits of decorating with pictures. "When choosing pictures, remember that you're not just filling up space on the wall. Don't be afraid to add an element of surprise, such as I have done with the unusual portrait of a black man in 18th-century costume which hangs in my London sitting room or the horribly graphic oil painting of people being eaten alive by lions." If his clients happen to have a lovely 18th-century painting or two, he will understand the need to show them off to their best advantage within the right decorative framework. For example, the colors in the room should always bow to the painting's color tones which will have naturally changed and darkened with age—especially noticeable in the whites. There must therefore be no pure white in the room because this would have the inevitable and unfortunate effect of making the picture look as if it is covered in soot. Naturally, the same rule applies to antique materials, an old piece of needlework, or a prized item of antique furniture whose wood has mellowed into a handsome patinated surface. If the client has a serious art collection, it becomes the principal consideration to be reflected in the choice of other decorative

A strong graphic effect is achieved by grouping pictures together in a block (left). The linen drapes, secured by tapes, (above) are a practical addition to stop the etchings from fading in sunlight.

The decorative value of pictures is greatly enhanced by placing them in conjunction with other objects in a carefully balanced arrangement (right).

"Blow up an image that you like on a color photocopier and frame it. Look for the unexpected or curiosities. It is so easy to get an instant effect now. But whatever you do, get away from those dreary little prints in dull little frames," he advises. In his own homes, he has an eclectic assortment of pictures, from the noble and rare to the positively idiosyncratic. There are miniatures and silhouettes, detailed prints of Persian noblemen and a vast oil painting of *The Durbar at Bharatpur* which suits the backdrop of Indian-esque

"Hang pictures in verticals or put up twenty watercolors to make a square. Never stagger pictures or make blocks of little pictures."

elements. Apart from color sensitivity in regard to general decorative effects, the window treatment, for example, should be simplified so as not to compete with the works of art for the attention of the viewer's admiring eye. Although one aspect of the scheme should not suffer because of another, nevertheless things of equal weight may be put together as long as the concepts are in sympathy.

In truth, Roger doesn't feel that fine paintings have to contribute to being a part of his decorative schemes. His advice is to use what you happen upon and whatever your imagination can conjure up in a thoughtful way. To him, the decorative effect and the little joke are the things that make a good picture.

Small pictures can be visually anchored by linking them together with ribbon or chain (above left), and sometimes the subject's decorative value may be increased by giving it a visually strong frame, such as the painted harlequin one below.

fabric on the walls. There is a small print of an Italian clown inside a frame decorated with a harlequin pattern, bought by Roger in Venice, and even some sheets of postage stamps framed in gilt-wood and standing on miniature table easels.

This is exactly the sort of thing that the early 20th-century artist Marcel Duchamp would have done: he became famous for his "Readymades," which were the kind of everyday objects that had no connection with art within the boundaries of their normal usage but became art when he placed them in a "gallery" context. Roger has achieved a similar effect with the stamps, which are seen as a repeat pattern, rather than distributed individually on envelopes and obscured by the

influenced by his sharp eye for graphic effects. The same "block" treatment has been applied to the arrangement of Gainsborough etchings shown on the previous pages. Their impact is greatly emphasized by their proximity to each other, while the plain frames do not detract from the content.

If you are dealing with a few select unrelated items, they should be hung in a way that considers the distribution of space between the objects, which is just as important as the objects themselves. Different players in the scene can relate to each other in perfect harmony because of the balance of space between them. Another way Roger likes to use smaller pictures is to hang them so that the vertical line is emphasized, particularly on either side of the fireplace. Of course, this is a traditional method of hanging but he uses a deliberately graphic distribution of shapes.

postage mark: here their graphic quality can be appreciated. The fragments of American homespun conform to this "Readymade" concept. These document pieces were originally simply woven as cloth samples, but they have now been given a place of honour on the wall of a client's home, hung together in individually framed segments to make one "picture."

When dealing with the arrangement of a number of related pictures on one wall, Roger suggests that they should be geometrically laid out, rather than staggered. "I like to hang pictures in vertical stripes or in squares so that you get a group of pictures framed together to make up a block," he explains. This style of framing is a good example of how his views on picture display and hanging are

Geometric emphasis is given by hanging rectangular and circular frames alternately (above right). The homespun samples (above left) and the sheet of stamps (below) are modern day "Readymades"—everyday objects presented as art.

Here, the geometric forms are alternated—circle, rectangle, circle, and so on—to add another dimension to the value of the works of art themselves.

Provided that the colors are not loud and the design not overbearing, patterned wall hangings make good backdrops to unrelated objects. This is illustrated in Roger's own drawing room, where pictures, among other objects, are hung on top of the fabric-draped walls. He also likes to hang pictures from open book shelves, replacing the serried ranks of photographs and ill-considered bits and pieces of random ornament he dislikes, but the pictures need to be a good strong shape so they don't get lost against the backdrop of books. He advocates hanging paintings up against the window or on a door and also likes the idea of an ever-changing scene. "I love the spontaneous and temporary feel of pictures propped up on the mantelshelf." This he has done in the Greens' dining room, where one Matisse line drawing leans against another, making a far more attractive arrangement than if the pictures had been hung on the wall. This offhand treatment reflects the casual and almost throwaway nature of the sketches perfectly.

Roger is amused by the visual stimulus of quirky, asymmetric displays from time to time and much admired such a grouping in an American client's home. When she first arrived in her country residence, there were not many pictures to fill the large amount of wall space, so she hung up an 18th-century carved wooden fire facing some way off the floor instead. As her collection of paintings grew, the partially painted fireplace remained to become an integral part of the arrangement. "When I entered the room for the first time, the fireplace hanging on the wall was the first thing I saw," Roger recalls. "It was filled with and surrounded by Gainsborough etchings, and the way she arranged those and some plates around them was utterly individual. I realized there and then that I had met a woman with great style."

Just as a fire facing becomes a "picture" without a fireplace, picture frames may be used as an amusing decorative device in their own right. This is illustrated in the entrance hall of the same house, where a tiny picture is set within an oversize frame. In Trudi Ballard's flat, a magnificent Rococo-style mirror frame is set off-center over the fireplace and is surrounded by a monochromatic display of creamware dishes. Of course, with Roger's fertile imagination, such scenes change from week to week, so what is here today may very well be gone tomorrow. But overall, he has a strong faith in the innovative ways people use pictures of all sorts. Pictures add individualism and expression to a home in a way that other, less personal, decorations cannot, so intimate is their identity. Choices are infinitely diverse, and there is something to suit everybody's taste and purse.

Pictures should interact with other elements in a room. Roger's instinct is to handle a picture according to its visual content rather than its monetary value or artistic pedigree. Here, one Matisse line drawing is casually propped up against another, their simple form being echoed by the attenuated lines in the humble arrangement of bare twigs on the table of this understated, beautifully crafted dining room.

Flowers

"I don't think one should over-flower a room." Roger's deceptively simple statement in fact says a great deal about his attitude to flower arranging. He has perfected a style that does away with flamboyance and artifice and focuses on the beauty of the individual flowers within their carefully chosen container. He uses flowers in a very different way from conventional florists: "big," "exotic," and "bold" are not adjectives that can be used to describe his arrangements. He has no enthusiasm for the gloriously self-conscious pedestal display in which the flowers sacrifice their own identity to the overall pizzazz of the mass. For him, a flower is chosen for its individual beauty, selected and matched to the right container so that they become inseparable contributors to the room's decorative story.

Flowers picked from the country roadside bring Roger more pleasure and artistic gratification than any exotic flower shop bloom. Lacy cow parsley, ephemeral cherry blossom, and sleek willow branches in tight bud will be collected by the armful on his way to or from his country home. A flower is never commonplace if it can be used to good effect in its new home, so white-flowered *Lamium*, the deadnettles which are far prettier—and friendlier—than their unkind cousins the stinging

Elongated "test tube" vases stylishly hold single blooms, as here with calla lilies (left). Roger's advice is that they should each have the same water level and be kept spotlessly clean.

Simple and favorite ways with flowers: mixed blooms of a single color in a lined basket (above) and the charm of a single bloom in a tiny vase (right).

Roger is a great believer in making flowers an intrinsic part of the smaller decorative scene, rather than making a louder solo statement. Anemones (above), snake's head fritillaries (below), chrysanthemums, cornflowers, mint, and a single old-fashioned rose (right) are all cut short in the stem to sit cozily with their heads nodding over the rims of their small containers.

Many of his arrangements are associated with blue-and-white containers and decorative objects, but not always. The froth of cherry blossom stems (opposite) showers forth from a painted Moroccan shopping basket.

nettles, heads of ripe wheat and the viciously yellow flowering rape are elevated to a place of worth among the floral battery. This broad field of taste for the common flower doesn't mean that he is in any way indiscriminate about his choices; indeed, he has very strong dislikes. But he is a great believer in making the best use of what is easily available around you, and he readily puts this into practice.

He has an extraordinary ability to hone in on just the thing that is needed. In the same way that he can spot the potential merit in a rusty lamp lurking in the depths of a junk shop, he can single out a simple wayside flower. With proper care and placement, both can be transformed. The kitchen and the supermarket are not excluded from his quest for plant material. Parsley is a great favorite to be used in emerald green bunches that explode from tiny blue-and-white vases or to sprout out of an ornamental elephant's how-dah, like a miniature tree canopy, or to be placed on the dining table in cut-down paper cups inside small silver beakers. Using that

"I hate expensive shop flowers. A whole bundle of old twigs in baskets can look better than an expensive orchid in a china cachepot."

British childhood favourite mustard and cress is another novel idea—one wonders if his guests are ever tempted to nibble his flower arrangements?—with which he creates a little lawn laid inside a lined, earth-filled rectangular basket.

Roger's fondness for countryside flowers—and edible greens for that matter—does not exclude all shop-bought or cultivated species. This would be far too restricting, considering that he is not a natural gardener, having neither the time nor the inclination for delving in the soil for the sake of propagation. Marguerites, anemones, and old roses are much loved for their pure charm, colors, and shape respectively; tulips are placed near a heat source to encourage them to open fully so they bow their heavy heads over the side of a painted basket; an ethereal green-and-white composition is made from the delicate sprays of the chrysanthemum called "Santini" combined prettily with chincherinchees and old roses. His preferred colors are soft shades of anything or just green and white, but he feels strongly that colors should

***Exotic flowers are rare** among Roger's floral battery, but he liked the shape of the red Singapore orchids (top left). Anemones fit so neatly into a small container that they are a popular choice (above), and an emerald green splash of parsley (right) is a favorite of his because of its humorous incongruity in formal arrangements.*

*"**Tall flowers and leaves make a contrast** with little pots of flowers," he says. Here he uses spiky willow and deep red gerberas to illustrate the statement. Whatever the flowers are, they should be replenished often—nothing looks sadder than neglected and drooping flowers.*

not be chosen simply to complement the color scheme of the room as this would compromise the choices of flower for the composition. This is particularly important in a blue-and-white scheme, something Roger would know all about. Blue and white is a color combination for which it is difficult to select appropriate flowers because of the lack of true blues in the floral spectrum (most "blue" flowers lean towards purple) and the resulting conflict mis-matched blues can create. Roger tends to stick with whites, or vivid greens when a shot of brightness is needed to lighten a scheme.

His displays are more influenced and focused by the shape of a flower than by its color and, indeed, his use of individual blooms requires a particular kind of flower to merit this special status. For example, lilies, especially *Lilium longifolium* and the calla lily, are ideal candidates for privileged treatment, placed in a single "test tube" vase or, even better, grouped together in triplicate. The linear shape and the strong flower outline allow them to perform as individuals without

in a sturdy basket, for example, and tuck in a few gladioli, or some such, and then plant flowering garlic and onions amid the flowers. He once did this with a mass of cow parsley so that his guests would think he was actually growing it indoors. When they made the expected exclamations of amazement, he confessed immediately that it was a ruse, but added, "I'm so glad you thought I had, anyway." This playful attitude even extends outdoors. One of his past assistants, Emma Burns, recalls the time when they sliced away at a great log basket to make it fit around a magnolia tree planted on the lawn so it would look as if the tree was growing out of it.

Roger does not turn up his nose at using artificial flowers. Indeed, he is not averse to using the occasional silk flower among leafy arrangements. "Black tulips and anything unusual, such as big white plastic calla lilies stuck among the leaves, can be fun in mid winter, if not convincing!" There is even a story, apocryphal perhaps, that he once planted blue plastic tulips outside the front door of his country home.

further embellishment, while the pure, clean lines of the vase enhance their singular beauty. As a rule, Roger does not like to see a tangle of stems in a clear glass vase, so the test tube container is the closest he comes to tolerating visible "legs". Instead, he will gather generous bunches of sweet peas or lily of the valley, hiding their stems in large china bowls. His usual method is to shorten the stems until the flowers are resting their chins on the rim of the container, whatever that may be. "Chop plants really short unless you're using tall stalks with leaves on, like viburnum or spring blossom. Most people make their flower arrangements too tall," says Roger firmly. This correlation of flower and container is crucial to the success of the final arrangement. Small containers should hold disproportionately large flowers.

Despite all his chopping and arranging and careful placement, Roger also loves flowers to look as if they are still growing, and is skilled at methods of disguise to make this artifice convincing. He will make a bed of peat

Colefax and Fowler
Showrooms and Stockists

For information about the furniture, fabrics, carpets, and trimmings shown in this book, please contact the Colefax and Fowler Press Office in London on 0171 493 2231.

Colefax and Fowler fabrics and wallpapers are available worldwide. For further information please contact the UK Sales and Export Sales Office or telephone 0181 874 6484.

Alternatively please contact one of the addresses below for the details of the distributors of Colefax and Fowler products nearest to you.

USA

Distributed through
Cowtan & Tout
D&D Building
10th Floor
979 Third Floor
New York
NY 10022
Telephone 212 753 4488
Fax 212 593 1839

For details of US showrooms telephone 212 647 6900.

UK

Colefax and Fowler
39 Brook Street
London W1Y 2JE
Telephone
0171 493 2231
Fax 0171 355 4037

Colefax and Fowler
110 Fulham Road
London SW3 6RL
Telephone
0171 244 7427
Fax 0171 373 7916

FRANCE

Colefax and Fowler
19 Rue du Mail
75002 Paris
Telephone
01 40 41 97 12
Fax 01 40 41 97 14

Acknowledgments

The publishers would like to thank Andrew Twort for the photographs of Valentino's house, and the following people for their various contributions: Sir Hardy Amies, Trudi Ballard, Mr. and Mrs. Peter Bentwood, Mr. and Mrs. Joe Bloom, Lady Boothby, Edward Bramson, Mr. and Mrs. Paul Brett, Jennifer Bristow, Emma Burns, Zoe Broadway, Nigel Cansfield, Philippa Clare, Eversheds, Stanley Falconer, Dorothy Fitchett, Valentino Garavani, Giancarlo Giammetti, Bridget Glasgow, Ann Grafton, Lady Grant, Mr. and Mrs. David Green, Guy Goodfellow, Ronald Gurney, Interior Workshops, Mr. and Mrs. Leonard Licht, Barrie McIntyre, Michael Raymond, Mrs. Mo Rothman, Mrs. Derald H. Ruttenberg, The Countess of Shelburne, Rebecca Streeter, Carlos Souza, Richard Timewell, Stephen Woodhams, William Yeoward, The Hon Lady de Zulueta.

Colefax and Fowler would like to thank the publishers, Ryland Peters & Small, the photographer James Merrell, the writer Suzanne Woloszynska, the editor Sian Parkhouse, and designer Larraine Shamwana for creating a book of vision, style and coherence.

Colefax and Fowler would like to specially thank Chester Jones for all his invaluable support, knowledge, and contribution.

$\mathcal{I}\,n\,d\,e\,x$

Figures in italics refer to picture captions.

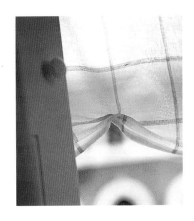